Sharing Faith in the Family

A Guide to Ritual and Catechesis

Sandra DeGidio, OSM

TWENTY-THIRD PUBLICATIONS
P.O. Box 180   West Mystic, CT 06388

Library of Congress Catalog Card Number 79-92544

ISBN 0-89622-119-9

Cover and interior design by Kay Leuschner
Cover art by Bette Baker and Mary Lou Rose
Interior art by Jeanne Bright
Editing by Kay Leuschner and Marie McIntyre

Dedicated to my parents and sister
who provided my first experience
of sharing faith in the family.

Contents

Introduction

Ten years ago I was a starving graduate student living on peanut butter sandwiches and black coffee, and trying to read everything from Early Church liturgies to Hemingway. Somewhere in the midst of that reading and writing a thesis on the attitude toward women in the literature of the Middle Ages, I was struck with what I was certain was divine inspiration—the concept of family religious education. I was convinced that I had become one of the 10 or 12 people in a generation who are truly creative, who really come up with a totally fresh and unique idea. Most of us who consider ourselves creative, you know, generally work from the germ of someone else's idea.

I began investigating and researching my "unique" idea. I read everything I could in the field of religious education. And, of course, as any truly creative person should, I spent hours lying on my bed, thinking, trying to determine where in my experience this majestic idea had been conceived.

Prior to my year at graduate school I had spent six years teaching upper elementary grades in Catholic schools. Those years also found me involved with Parish CCD programs, CCD teacher training, and the beginnings of family sacramental preparation programs which were then being developed.

Hindsight is such an enlightening thing. As I searched my memory, I found myself feeling angry at the recollection of parents dropping their children off for someone else to "teach them their religion." I began resenting the "why-can't-the-Church-teach-my-kids-about-the-sacraments?" attitude from those early parent meetings. I even began feeling guilty at having been a part of an institution which had spent millions of dollars trying to teach children something they were in no way able to comprehend, while assuming, at least indirectly, that parents were incapable of transmitting any religious values to their children. I was disturbed by an attitude which seemed to me to be prevalent—that the Catholic school and the institutional Church had the monopoly on religious education.

The last three years I taught, I found myself angered even more by the fact that I was in a parish in which two-thirds of the budget went into a Catholic school for 150 students while virtually nothing went into a CCD program for over 500 students. Adult education was not even considered. The great boast of the CCD progam was that "they always broke even" by having the children buy their own textbooks. Somehow, it seemed to me that the family sacramental preparation programs held tremendous promise for the future of religious education. All that seemed to be needed was people with vision to further develop the basic aims of those programs.

With all of these feelings welling up in me, I read Gabriel Moran's *Vision and Tactics,* in which the author seemed to agree with me. Then I found a book that really made my head spin with delirious joy, *Children, Church and God* by Robert O'Neil and Michael Donovan! It was a book that was eight years ahead of its time. The book was subtitled *The Case Against Formal Religious Education.* In reading and re-reading it, I began to put my experiences in perspective and to see how the authors were leading me into the realm of family religious education. Dolores Curran gave me the next great hope in the development of this idea. Her book *Who, Me Teach My Child Religion?* helped convince me that the family was capable indeed of transmitting the faith, even in the absence of structured aid from the Church.

It seemed to follow then, that with aid, the family probably could be the best teacher of religious attitudes, values and goals. Had not Vatican II shown us that we were a Church of creative people? Had not that same Council stated: "Since parents have conferred life on their children, they have a most solemn obligation to educate their offspring in the Faith"? Were we not receiving a mandate to aid parents in their "most solemn obligation"?

My "unique" idea was beginning to take on a logical rationale. I called the pastor with whom I would be working as a pastoral associate in northern Wisconsin the following year and presented my idea. He was not only open but began preparing the parishioners for it.

Then it happened! My research finally led me to the realization that my idea was neither fresh nor unique. Looking at the history of religious education in the Catholic, Jewish, and Protestant traditions revealed to me that it had been done in the past, albeit in radically different sociological situations. Families had shared and passed on their faith since day one. Furthermore, some few communities, especially around the Midwest, were following the same basic rationale and were beginning to develop family religious education programs.

Having picked up my wounded ego, finished my thesis, passed my comprehensive exams, packed my car and headed north, I began my new career with families. After two years in rural northern Wisconsin, I came to the Parish Community of St. Joseph, a 1700-family suburban parish in New Hope, Minnesota, just west of Minneapolis. Here I designed, developed and implemented family religious education for five years.

This book comes out of that career experience. It is written with the hope that some of the research I am fortunate to have done, and the experience which I am fortunate to have had will be of aid to the many pastoral teams, DRE's and priests across the country who are trying so hard to help family faith sharing become more natural for American families.

The book will not offer a tailored, packaged program to be picked up and reproduced for any and every parish, but hopefully it will offer many "germs of ideas" which creative people can pick up and build upon. *Creativity* is perhaps the most important ingredient in the design and development of family programs in parishes.

Hopefully, it will be both practical enough to be of aid to parishes just beginning to develop some form of family religious education, and theoretical enough to challenge continued research and development of further family ministry in parishes that have already begun family religious education. The family is still the finest learning center for the maturing person—both adult and child. It is within the family circle, better than in the best of schools, that each family member learns the basic human and Christian values. And it is within the community of believers that the affirmation for those values can be provided to aid people's maturation processes.

If some of what follows sounds strongly didactic, please bear with me. The statements come out of strong convictions which I not only believe firmly, but which, in many cases I have seen proven, particularly with the help of the families and pastoral team at St. Joseph's. I have been fortunate to have been allowed to design family programs for two parishes. I have had opportunities to make some mistakes, and have enjoyed many small and some large successes. I am confident that you will take these convictions, failures, successes, add your own experience, research and creativity, examine the needs of families in your area, and together, we can continue to minister to those basic social and religious units of every society—the families in our parishes.

The family is still the finest learning center for the maturing person — both adult and child. It is within the family circle, better than in the best of schools, that each family member learns the basic human and Christian values.

There are few, if any, family faith sharing experiences which fail.

As with almost every book, there are people without whom this book could not have been. Hopefully, they are people like myself who love to read the acknowledgment sections of books and will be pleased to know that something of themselves is between these covers. I would like to thank them publicly.

First of all, the manuscript would never have contained correctly spelled words and neat, readable typing without Sister Katherine Stoffel and her magic typewriter. The book may never have contained more than theoretical babble without the parishioners, pastor and staff of the Parish Community of St. Joseph who had the courage to risk with me and who encouraged me to write it all down, and the Webster Area Catholic Community and their pastor, Reverend Ed Senn, for allowing me to work through many of the rough spots in the theory with them.

Special thanks, too, go to Jim Bitney, Dean Dolan and Mike Joncas who will find much of themselves and their creativity between these covers. My religious community deserves many thanks for their support and for allowing me the time to write, while at the same time keeping me from having to live the image we all have of the "starving writer."

Then there are those who provided special support and encouragement—Theresa Sandok, Julie Strzok, Mary Alice Willems, Tom Robertson, Jane Charette, and Dolores Curran. I often wonder how many times I might have given up the process of this book without them. And finally, thanks are due to Kathie Power and the families of St. Joseph's Parish who helped me prove that a family catechetical program which is based on sound theory and is well organized can continue and grow when a new director takes it over.

Chapter 1

The Stone of Sisyphus in Religious Education

Let's Look for a Better Way

Religious education has long been both the triumph and the tribulation of the American Church. We cannot deny that former methods of religious education responded to a need of a particular time, sometimes effectively. But society has changed, needs are different and many older models of religious education are no longer effective for contemporary needs. Since the late 50's and early 60's, religious educators have been trying to redefine and re-program educational ministries. The question is, have we looked, searched, and programmed in the right direction?

We have inherited from the past three concepts of religious education which I contend are no longer valid. The first is a concept of education which concentrates mainly on transmitting religious information. It produces a model of instruction in a school setting with teacher imparting knowledge—or less fully, facts—to the students. The second concept is related in that it is centered on the transmitting of that religious information exclusively to children under the assumption that they can assimilate the knowledge, and that they need only knowledge in order to be good Christians. Finally, we have worked from a concept which umbrellas the other two —namely, we have confused *religion* with *faith*. Religious education is far more than any or all of these concepts.

Religious education, correctly understood, is *not* synonymous with schooling, with children, or with religion. John Dewey, one of the educational giants of our century, insisted that all of life educates. This could not be more true in terms of religious education. Un-

fortunately we have categorized parish life into education, liturgy, social action and pastoral activity.

We read much that counteracts such division, but the distinction remains and will remain, as long as we continue to see religious education as a means of teaching people about Christianity as opposed to integrating the total parish life and helping people live Christian life more fully. Until we have a vision of the interrelatedness of total parish life, until we work together as parish ministers, we are going to be doomed to roll the educational stone of Sisyphus.*

Education in general, and religious education in particular, is a *process* of development and growth involving all formal and informal methods of transmitting beliefs, attitudes, values, behaviors, skills, sensibilities, appropriate knowledge, and most of all, in the case of religious education, *faith*. Religious education has most to do with persons growing and developing in the faith we call Christian. It is much more than a process of transmitting content to someone.

In an attempt to break out of this instruction model, we moved from using an outline of doctrine (the catechism) as a text, to models which confused the teaching of religion with the teaching of art. Our main resources in those days were old *Life* magazines, scissors, paste and crayons. We have gone the media route, the sensitivity, touchy-feely, magic

---

*Sisyphus was a legendary king who was doomed by the gods to roll a huge stone up a hill only to have it roll down again and again just before it reached the top.

circle path, and the liturgy line, trying to make our Eucharistic worship ritual serve as our total education.

In all of these efforts, our underlying intent was to teach experientially. To facilitate our goal, we promoted smaller classes, more teachers, creative dramatics, and terrific texts. We even went the route of family education because we were convinced that religious edu-

---

Religious education is much more than transmitting content.

---

cation without the reinforcement of the home was meaningless. Still, in all of our programming, we concentrated on resources which transmitted information. We attempted to teach people *about* Christianity, rather than work at sharing our faith and living Christianity with them.

John Westerhoff III so accurately points out in his book *Will Our Children Have Faith?* that since the turn of the century, the Church has followed the schooling/instruction paradigm of American society under the erroneous assumption that it could be the panacea for all our problems. Somehow, in launching so vigorously into such a specific and very limited form of education, we overlooked the initial purpose and intent both of the CCD model of religious education and the Sunday School concept adhered to by Protestant Churches.

We spent too little time sharing faith with people and helping them share faith with one another, and too much time trying to teach people all *about* Christianity. I did this for years, because *I* was the knowledgeable person with information in my head to impart. *They* had, after all, hired me to teach them all the marvelous things I knew that they didn't know. Now, with hindsight, I question how much faith I shared with all those people, be-

cause I was so concerned about teaching them all I knew about religion.

As long as our parish education goals remain primarily centered around the communication of content, doctrine or knowledge, we are doomed to failure. The goal of religious education is *persons* who are continually growing and are able to respond openly to life and radically to Christ. We need to look together at what it means to be Christian, and we need to center our goals on sharing faith with people rather than sharing knowledge. We need to distinguish the *heart* of the Christian message from the peripheral details.

There are those who have made the distinction between *religious education* and *religious socialization* in an attempt to rationalize their way through the dilemma. The distinction has some validity, but again, it promotes a categorical situation, separating where religious socialization stops and religious education begins. According to this rationale, religious socialization is the formal and informal influences through which persons acquire their understanding and ways of living (values, attitudes, behavior, sensibilities). Religious edu-

---

It has most to do with persons growing and developing in the faith we call Christian.

---

cation, then, becomes all the deliberate, systematic and sustained efforts to transmit or evolve knowledge which supports one's attitudes, values, behavior and sensibilities.

Religious education, tends, in this type of distinction, to become a highly complex indoctrination and initiation into a subculture, rather than into religious *faith*. It remains synonymous with schooling and is only a specific and very limited form of the numerous ways in which people grow in an understanding of, comfort with, and knowledge of their faith.

The distinction is often carried one step further, in terms of family-centered religious education. Parishes develop family programs to aid religious socialization while having other programs of religious education to teach religion.

Unfortunately, in both cases we are working from an instruction model which enables adults to be with children in ways that encourage the adult to assert power over the child. Parents concerned about family education are constantly trying, whether at home or at church, to do something *for* their children, when they should instead, be concerned about doing *with* them, particularly with sharing faith in and outside the family boundaries.

Henri Nouwen, in his book *Creative Ministry* makes a marvelous distinction between violent and redemptive learning/teaching. Violent learning he describes as competitive. There is a desperate need to succeed, to come away with some knowledge. It is unilateral. Someone, usually the teacher, is competent and knowledgeable, and someone else, the student, is not. And finally, violent learning, according to Nouwen, is alienating. The learning is directed outward, outside the learning situation. The student must wait for a later opportunity in the *real* world to put the information to use.

Redemptive learning, on the other hand, Nouwen points out, is evocative. There is a natural sharing of strengths, weaknesses, desires, and needs among those involved. It is bilateral in that there is learning from one another. No one person is the expert. Redemptive learning, moreover, is actualizing. Through the natural exchange of ideas, information, and faith, the objective is not to become prepared for life later, but it is the lived experience here and now. Nouwen maintains that violent learning reaps non-learning, whereas redemptive learning creates new life styles. (I blush to think about how much violent teaching I have done under the guise of redemption and nonviolence.)

> **As long as our parish education goals remain primarily centered around the communication of content, doctrine or knowledge, we are doomed to failure.**

Nouwen's descriptions reflect very clearly, to me, the distinction between religious education and religious development. In our usual concept of religious education involving teacher and students, content to be covered, age/grade groupings etc., students are expected to learn something rather than change or be enabled to develop in faith. The emphasis is put on *the material* rather than on *persons*. In this redemptive learning concept, there is little if any concern about material or information to pass on. The emphasis is on persons and those persons challenging, aiding and affirming one another in their faith growth. The fascinating thing is that in such learning, information is, in fact, transmitted. But the information is immediately meaningful and life-giving.

To think that a change in terminology can change attitudes is simplistic, but I do believe that such a linguistic change can help, especially if there is a clear understanding of the terms being employed. Education has become too narrow a concept in our society, and I would therefore propose that it is a term that ought to be used only to refer to the gaining of knowledge and understanding about religion.

Those of us who are religious "educators" tend to see our ministry as much broader than that (or at least we should). We are concerned with sharing faith, with supporting that growing faith, with conversion, with the following of Christ, with the living of beliefs. That being true then, I think we would do well to consider Berard Marthaler's distinction between religious education and catechesis. The two are not synonymous. Marthaler suggests that religious education is basically an academic endeavor, while catechesis is a pastoral activity intended to share the faith of the Church and to aid that faith in becoming a living, conscious, and active ingredient in the life of a maturing person and a maturing community.

ior. It is concerned with helping individuals and communities answer the question: "What is it to be Christian today?" There is a time for the sharing of knowledge about Christianity; there is a time (I would propose constantly) for religious socialization; there are even times when the two can happen simultaneously.

Education is not ministry because of the na-

The aim of catechesis is to initiate persons into a community with its own story, memories, understandings, values, actions, and rituals.

The aim of catechesis is to initiate persons into a community with its own story, memories, understandings, values, actions and rituals. It aims at aiding those persons in the internalizing of that community's faith and helping them to adopt that faith as their own. Catechesis helps people individually and as a community to develop communion with God and with one's fellow and sister human beings. Its content is not the scope and sequence of doctrine, not institutional religion, not knowledge of Jesus, but faith in Jesus. It is a life's work because it is very much related to conversion which is an ever-recurring phenomenon in the life of the individual Christian and the Christian Community.

Catechesis is the pastoral activity which brings understanding to the realm of appreciation. We would do well in the Church today to try to inspire greater appreciation and less understanding. As someone has so aptly said: "Christianity is more a poem than a syllogism; the Church is more an experience than an institution."

Like education, catechesis is deliberate, intentional, systematic and based on interpersonal interacting. But it is interested in more than knowing and understanding. It is especially concerned with commitment and behav-

ture of the educational process but because of what we really claim to be in the light of the Gospel, and what we really live. The question becomes, then, is schooling/instruction as necessary as we have made it in the Christian community for religious development to take place? Or is living as a Christian with others inherently religious development? If we attend to being Christian with one another, if we attend to the pastoral activity of catechesis for the total community, need we attend to such concern for schooling and instruction?

For our purposes, then, we shall use the term catechesis rather than religious education. We shall see it as a pastoral action, as sharing and experiencing with others rather than as some *thing* we want someone else to *know*.

The second attitude which we have inherited from the past and which I would suggest is equally invalid is that religious education is primarily, if not exclusively, concerned with *children*. If one's concept of religious formation is based upon a schooling/instruction model, then it follows that religious development will concentrate on children in the same way that our social structure links schooling and education with children.

However, Christianity is a religion for

adults. Soren Kierkegaard in the mid-nineteenth century made a similar observation regarding Christianity and the teaching of religion. In his *Concluding Unscientific Postscript,* he examines the problems: "What is a Christian?" and "How am *I* to become a Christian?" He maintains that to become a Christian, to be a Christian is a very difficult thing and he makes a definite distinction be-

We throw in a little role playing to create a guise of experiential learning. We concentrate our educational efforts on goals of understanding ideas instead of on living Christianity with our children. We seem convinced that children ought at least to be exposed to certain truths, and we state, "that children ought to be introduced to and taught the basics of Scripture, of the nature of God, of the con-

---

It aims at aiding those persons in the internalizing of that community's faith and helping them to adopt that faith as their own.

---

tween truly adult Christianity and childish Christianity, childish Christianity being non-Christianity, and merely myth and idolatry.

In his conclusion, he says: "Just as Christianity did not come into the world during the childhood of humankind but in the fullness of time, so, too, in its decisive form it is not equally appropriate to every age in man's life. . . . To cram Christianity into a child is something that cannot be done, for it is a general rule that everyone comprehends only what he has use for, and the child has no decisive use for Christianity. . . . The Christianity which is taught to a child . . . is not properly Christianity but idyllic mythology. It is childishness in the second power."* That was in the nineteenth century, before Piaget, Kohlberg, Goldman or Fowler and all that we now know about child development, faith development, moral development and religion readiness.

Much has been said and said often about the *futility* of trying to teach children *about* Christianity. Yet we continue to waste our time at it, and we write out lesson plans with objectives such as: "To show the students that the members of Christ's Kingdom live and work in the present because of their hope in the future fulfillment of the Kingdom."

cept of Church, of sacramentality, and of morality."

Such an emphasis on doctrine is a backlash of the Reformation and the supposed need for an apologetic theology so that the Protestant "heresy" would not "gobble up our children." Somehow we have continued to believe that if children know certain prayers and those "basics," all will be well for them the rest of their lives and they will not "fall away" from the Church. So what happens when we try to teach them these things?

We have opted to deal with the content of faith "historically," because that is how God chose to reveal God. But less vapidly, we have been teaching the content of faith historically because all people, children included, are interested in history, interested in the present historical evolution from which genuine life emerges.

It is true children are interested in history—their own history. The all important elements of history, however, are rarely understood by the majority of elementary-aged children. Therefore, if we look upon the teaching of Scripture to children as transmitting a past set of revealed truths by which we live (as I'm afraid we often do), we deny true history and make some sort of idol out of the past.

Similarly, if we encourage young Christians to live in the present, and to have their hopes in the future, but point their minds toward the past where, supposedly, all revealed truth lies (which incidentally, is a gross misconception of revelation), no new and personal questions or answers are made possible for the children. With such a sense of history we discourage exploration of God for them and they become bored. How often this is the case in our teaching of religion to children!

A friend of mine tells the story of her five-year-old who was "playing with numbers" one day and came to her with the equation "7-9 = -2" written on a piece of paper. My friend, not looking carefully, having a preconceived, firmly fixed notion of what a five-year-old ought to be able to comprehend, proceeded to explain that the equation was wrong and that the 7 and 9 should be reversed. The child in exasperation explained the equation, pointing out the minus sign in front of the 2, which the mother had not noticed.

We often do the same in religious education. We come with our tunnel vision, our prepared lesson plans based on our set models of what children ought to learn, and proceed to explain away any desire the child might have to explore God or our faith. In a very real sense, we destroy any further desire on the part of the child to develop any personal relationship with us or with a Supreme Being.

History, in essence, is a very personal thing. At the same time it is an abstraction, containing within itself the notions of temporal dimensions, causality, social forces, personal motivations, and not simply facts. Therefore, we do not expect the fourth grader to grasp the dilemma of a John Kennedy in facing the Crisis of the Bay of Pigs, but then inconsistently we do present the child with the dilemma of Abraham in sacrificing his son. Likewise, we tell the children, Jesus lived then, he did thus and so, and he wants us to live as he did. But Jesus is full of paradoxes which children cannot comprehend, and the essence of Christianity is full of abstractions which are equally impossible for the child to understand prior to age 12 or 13.

According to the various catechetical directories which have passed our desks since Vatican II, the goal of any religious education program is the child's learning about God and God's nature. This is a difficult task indeed. The child can understand the entity we name God only in the simplest manner, i.e., God is a person, with a body, a voice, with emotions. Their most common questions about God are deeply personal: "Does God cry?" "What's God's middle name?" "How does God get food?" "How old is God?"

To try to explain the nature of God to children, we proceed to immerse them in sense experiences (experiential learning). This is a good way to increase children's sense awareness; however, it is a decidedly poor way to explain the existence of God. The young child will be strongly anthropomorphic in his/her thinking about God, thinking of God as a Superman—but still a man—with magical powers.

This makes it even more difficult to understand the relationship between God and Jesus. Here there is a confusion and interchangeability of names, Jesus having the same human characteristics as God, his powers being those of God, because, of course, we must teach the miracles of Jesus, even though the exegesis accompanying them, and their deeper meaning, are beyond a child's comprehension. Consequently, the relationship between God and Jesus becomes one of master magician and apprentice. The Holy Spirit becomes something like Casper the Friendly Ghost, sort of there in the background to lend a hand when we are in trouble. So much for the teaching of the nature of God, the basic of our faith, to children.

The term *community* or *community of faith* is used both in the catechetical directories and in most parish philosophies of education, and is the basis for any proper understanding of Church. Most elementary-aged children have great difficulty going beyond the bonds of persons to the notion of community, and seeing that actions and decisions have consequences which are communal, rather than merely personal.

In order to comprehend the idea of community in any adequate manner, children must be able to conceptualize in what ways various functions are related to one another, to common ends, and to the community as a whole. The organizing principle or focus or center of these functions must be abstracted, for if it is not, the functions or parts will be perceived as independent, unrelated, and self-contained.

the same time, this type of passing on of values and attitudes is really a type of sociocultural initiation for children, rather than the formulation of any mature freedom, which is the essence of Christian morality and possible only in conjunction with a mature faith.

I should like to propose that any doctrinal teaching or learning for the elementary-aged child is nigh to impossible, not unlike swim-

---

The best education takes place when there is first of all a question; yet we concentrate so completely on teaching answers — before the questions have been asked.

Children, lacking a differentiated view of the social order, cannot grasp the needs, present and future, of the total community.

As we go beyond the concept of community and speak of a faith community, the resulting problems are compounded geometrically. For example, if children are unable to understand the notion of community, upon which any proper understanding of the Church must be based, how can they begin to appreciate the ideas of sacramentality, which itself depends upon a notion of Church? If a notion of sacrament as a special kind of community action of the Church is unintelligible, how can children learn about the sacraments proper? If children lack a realistic sense of history, what sense can they make out of the whole fabric of salvation history?

Given these difficulties, what remains of the entire body of doctrinal content we propose to give to our children? Not much, it would seem. So why do we continue to impart such an ideological superstructure to children? Our seldom acknowledged justification is a hoped-for dividend we term "proper moral behavior," the kinds of attitudes and actions that are approved by parents, reinforced by the Church and totally in the realm of parent education, not institutional education. At

ming in an ocean of Vaseline. By attempting to teach children doctrinal concepts, we run the risk of transmitting idolatrous notions of God, poor historical, theological foundations; and we tend to immunize children from religious inquiry, thus destroying the best possibilities for real religious learning at the appropriate times.

We are aware that the best education takes place when there is first of all a question; yet we concentrate so completely on teaching answers—before the questions have been asked. We inundate our children with blank verse incantations about many concepts that are unintelligible to them. We give children too much too soon.

Consequently, when young people (adolescents) begin to ask the kind of questions which are the core of religious inquiry, when as Fowler and Westerhoff point out, they are in the stage of "searching faith," they often abandon these misconceptions of religion learned earlier, throwing out a premature baby (the faith) with the bath (poor historical, theological concepts). Therefore, the Christianity they reject is one they never learned to know at all, simply because they were unable to know it as children. But they thought they did, and so did we.

The answer to our dilemma is not necessarily the total abandonment of catechesis for the elementary-aged child, though we should abandon any attempts to teach doctrine, no matter how subtle they may be. Instead, we should begin, or continue, to relate our children to the powerful symbols of the faith in a vivifying ritualizing lifestyle. Ritual is the meeting place of the past and present. It is liv-

time, but not rejecting Christianity. In working with each of these young people, I asked that they begin worshiping with the community and that they participate in some of our regularly scheduled youth programs in order to become acquainted with other young people their age in the community. I also set up a course of individual study selecting current catechetical material in keeping with their age

---

We've spent too little time sharing faith with people and helping them share faith with one another, and too much time trying to teach people all about Christianity.

---

ing tradition. Ritual will be a key element in each step of the religious development process of the elementary-aged child. For in ritual, the child lives the truths of our faith. Therefore, we ought to play with children creatively, worry less about what they know doctrinally, and concern ourselves more with developing an appreciation of the faith. We will approach religion more as an art to be appreciated than as a science to be analyzed. This is what the younger child is equipped to do best—live in the now, enjoy life and play. Then, later, when mental abilities develop which are more attuned to the abstract, they will be able to enjoy investigating, researching, examining, weighing, scrutinizing, and meditating on those basics of scripture, the nature of God, the concept of the Church, of sacraments and of morality. And they will enjoy such academic activity as adolescents if they have not been inundated with all the doctrinal words as younger children. They will not respond to our efforts with "I've heard that all before."

Recently, in our parish, we had some twelve- to sixteen-year-olds surface who had not been baptized or formally educated religiously. In every case, it was a situation of parents rejecting institutional religion for a

and background. They were incorporated into the year-long process of the adult rites of initiation in our parish, sharing with the groups of adults who were preparing to make a profession of faith on Holy Saturday and participating in the rites of the stages of initiation with the other catechumens.

There is no comparison between the enthusiasm with which those young people approached theology and the lack of enthusiasm which most young people their age have for the same information. Those youngsters were full of questions and eager to try to determine answers. In every case, they sought baptism because they wanted to belong to a community that believed what they thought they would like to believe. And inevitably, before the process of initiation was completed, they asked if they could receive Eucharist with the community before they were officially received into the Church.

In one case, using the Socratic method, a thirteen-year-old was able to figure out for himself all seven sacraments and their basic meanings. I gave him the simple definition that sacraments are celebrations of high points in the life of a Christian, that they are opportunities for us, with other members of the Christian community, to encounter the

Lord through symbols and actions. We had already talked some about what baptism meant and he had recently participated in a communal anointing of the sick. With that background and experience along with a few questions from me, he proceeded with ease to determine the other five.

Working with those young people was one of the most exhilarating and at the same time depressing things I have ever done. The exhilaration is obvious, but it was depressing because I knew that for the most part we had and were continuing to immunize hundreds of other youngsters from such genuine inquiry at an appropriate age. I believe that it is neither necessary nor moral to subject our children to that type of religious immunization.

This brings us to our third error in terms of religious development—our confusion between faith and religion. We have tended to equate the two, when in fact, there is a definite distinction between religion and faith. Faith is something deeply personal, dynamic, ultimate. It is that which prompts the things we do which are religious. Religion, however, is best equated with institutions—formalized creeds, theologies, moral codes. In short, religion provides for us the communal means and methods by which we express our faith which is much deeper than any creed, any statement, any religious act. Learning about religion is an intellectual activity. Faith can never be solely intellectual. Faith is deeper than all of its expressions. Faith, as life, is organic. That is, it grows and changes and develops. Faith, as life, is an end or goal—all our efforts are ultimately to maintain and enhance its maturation.

But we have made religion the end. Religion is important but not ultimate; religion is a *means* to the *end*. Religion has become the end of our educational ministry because we can teach about religion, we can measure and evaluate objectively how much religion we have taught. We can determine the scope and sequence of our texts; we can break it down into concepts to be presented. Faith cannot be dissected and measured.

Indeed, faith cannot be taught by any method. We can live in faith, we can grow in faith, we can act in faith, we can share our faith with one another. We can celebrate our faith, ritualize our faith, but we cannot give another person our faith. We can, however, give another person a set of religious principles, which without a living faith become something filed away, often to be discarded later. We have, in a sense, taught all sorts of

The goal of religious education is to grow continually and to respond openly to life and radically to Christ.

religious actions and creeds when there was only a very immature faith to prompt those actions. Consequently, for many whom we have taught, religion became meaningless or religion became the ultimate with very little, if any, reason for its existence.

To use a limping analogy, we have taught all of the techniques and rudiments of swimming on the edge of the pool, never inviting the learner to plunge in, never plunging in ourselves to share the realities and exhilaration of the water. The result is that when the learner finds himself/herself in the water he/she is unable to correlate the facts with the lived experience. There is a great difference between learning the strokes and swimming. Likewise, there is a great difference between learning all about religion and living the faith. We have so concerned ourselves with quantifiable religion that we have lost a sense of the quality of people's faith-life, which is of much greater import and significance.

We education ministers have been like Sisyphus, that legendary king who was doomed for all eternity to continuously roll a huge stone to the top of an immense hill in Hades, only to have it roll down each time just a few feet from the top. Each of our new techniques over the years was going to be our best educational method yet, remember? The methods might have been good, but our premises were erroneous and so was our end. Assuming an educational model centered on children, and making religion our end make our efforts as *futile* as those of Sisyphus. Likewise, separating religious education from the totality of the community's life, making education a preparation for life rather than a sharing in that life means that, like Sisyphus, we separate our-selves from any one who can help us roll that stone to its destination.

Family or intergenerational catechesis could very well be the model which can break through the cycle in which we find ourselves caught, but we have to let go our "safe and secure" models, risk new models and ask families to risk with us. It can work as I shall demonstrate in later chapters.

Religion is important but not ultimate; religion is a means to the end.

Chapter 2

Developing Family Programs

Seven Necessary Steps to Success

Family catechesis, or family-centered religious education as it is most commonly referred to, is a programming phenomenon that has occurred in the Church over the past five years. The development of family-centered programs appears concurrently with the heightening alarm about the health of the North American family and at the same time with a cry to get "back to basics" in religious education. If we attune ourselves to both of these situations and are open to some risks, family catechesis could very well be our present and future hope.

I see family catechesis as an attempt to strengthen and affirm parents in their rightful positions as mediators of values and attitudes, and to equip them to share Christian faith with their children in the context of their sharing life together and recognizing God's presence in their lives. It takes place most often through structured experiences or programs. Family catechesis is essentially adult-centered, and its focus is the sharing of faith rather than doctrine.

The adult-centeredness is based on the new understandings that contemporary psychology and sociology bring to bear on family living and on fresh interpretations of tradition that theologians and catechists are articulating.

More and more psychologists and sociologists working with individual persons are now realizing that every person exists within a system of relationships—the most primary being the family. The health and growth of the person is therefore strongly influenced by those others who also make up the system; and vice versa, the one necessarily affects the others. This systems approach further maintains that

a family is only as healthy as the adults in that family, because adults create the family and establish the norms by which the family members will develop and grow.

Theologians are bringing us to fresh implications of the traditional belief that being Christian is an incarnational way of life. Faith involves the total person and happens in real lived situations. One of the most human situations is, of course, the family. The most actualizing transmission of faith takes place in the family, through its rituals of life, of meal sharing, of interrelationships, of recreation, and of regular prayer and worship celebrations.

The center of faith has always been the family. It is just that we forgot that for awhile and now have a need to remind ourselves and build systems, or re-inforce processes whereby the faith can be genuinely passed on from generation to generation. Family catechesis might well be considered a neo-traditional catechetical approach.

Thus we are experiencing a return to the basics, pointed to by various professions and disciplines. The basic we return to is that parents are not only the primary, but the best influences on their children's faith growth and their religious and moral development. Another basic is that the best religious education is casual and organic. It grows out of reflection on one's lived experience, which happens most frequently within the family and forms an integral part of the whole called community. Catechesis which is organic cannot be structured into simulated experiences but rather occurs in a real situation which calls for action and response. It occurs when there is a question and when that question is answered with a response which expresses not only fact but the faith in relation to that fact—catechesis occurs in what is often called the *teachable moment*.

Family catechesis, then, is basically adult-centered. The parish's greatest contribution to families is through its work with parents. Aiding them in their growth, affirming and supporting them in their roles as parents and transmitters of the faith is our most important task in the designing and implementing of family programs. If parents are secure in their faith, if we help them to live that faith life, ritualize it, be aware of the numerous teachable moments they have every day, then the faith will indeed be passed on to the next generation.

That all seems simple, but how do we go about doing that through our programming on the parish level? I suggest a simple seven step process:

Seven Step Process

1. Assess needs with the people of your parish.
2. Convince your pastor or pastoral team of the need for family catechesis.
3. Define the areas of need and concern.
4. Pre-evangelize for family catechesis.
5. Set goals and objectives.
6. Design your program.
7. Implement your program.

The steps seem coldly administrative listed that way. Developing family programs can be neither cold nor purely administrative. Perhaps examining each of the steps will help.

1. Assess Needs

We begin by talking with parents. When I came to St. Joseph's Parish Community six years ago, I was hired specifically to develop and implement a family-centered program. The parish had a five-year history of making adult education a priority; they had already done much of what I like to call the pre-evan-

gelization for family catechesis, and had a children's religious education program of about 20 hours a year. The day I arrived, the pastor handed me a sheet of paper with a short paragraph requesting more CCD for children, with 40 names, addresses and phone numbers on it. "These people are going to give you the most trouble," he said. "They want a structured CCD program for their kids."

Having learned just two years before that one does not win friends, influence people and develop a successful family program by storming into a parish with an expertly designed program, I decided that perhaps these 40 couples could be of help in my assessing the needs of families in the parish. Only after that was done could I begin to design a program. It is eminently ridiculous to develop a program before understanding what families believe are their needs. They usually know better than we what their needs are. They, after all, have the families, know what their problems are, what successes and failures they have had, what visions and hopes they have, in what directions they would like to grow as families. Furthermore, if there are families who are not aware of their needs, the process of assessment can aid them in recognizing what it is that might help them. Needs can be surfaced by simply asking critical questions.

There are any number of ways to assess parish needs: questionnaires, group meetings, small group information gatherings, a census-type process, personal visits, etc. I prefer the personal visit method. The informal conversation technique of simply sitting down in people's homes and talking with them has been most effective for me. Three aspects present themselves in such encounters that do not exist in the other assessment methods. First of all, the family members feel important and special because someone from the parish is taking the time to sit down and listen to them. They feel a sense of worth and will usually be very open in expressing their thoughts and feelings.

Secondly, this method enables us to get to know several families. We meet them in the atmosphere which is most comfortable to them, their homes. Usually there is a sharing of food and drink which adds to the sense of calm and relaxation. My sister maintains that one of the things she learned growing up in an Italian family is that sharing food can alleviate almost any anxiety for the moment. Once we have eaten with someone, our relationship is different, usually closer, more trusting and certainly less formal.

questionnaire but the returns will be greater and more satisfying for all concerned.

Finally, the third reason for my preference of this mode of assessment is that it provides opportunity for clarification of statements. I approach the visit with some definite questions to encourage expression of needs, questions such as: *What could the parish do to help you as a family . . . you as a parent? Do you know what your children are doing in*

Growing families will not remain in a parish that shows no evidence of a community spirit, that celebrates liturgies like the turning of a prayer wheel, that has little pastoral concern for people, and has little or no involvement in social justice.

We have to realize that when we begin talking to parents about the faith growth of their children, they often are apprehensive. Both society and the Church have in many ways caused parents to lose confidence in themselves and be discouraged about their inadequacy. Lacking self-confidence, parents have turned to the helping professions: the teachers, psychologists, sociologists, counselors, social workers and the clergy and religious. They hesitate to get deeply involved in their children's growth, development and upbringing, and relinquish their rights as parents to those whom they think can do a better job than they. Unfortunately, then, their children become shaped primarily by advertisers, peers and "professionals."

Parents are not always pleased with the outcome but have difficulty believing that they could do any better.

The personal visit over coffee and cookies provides the environment for such fears to be expressed, and also provides the opportunity to begin alleviating those fears. This method takes much more time than making out a

their religion classes? Does your family find enough time to do the things its members would like to do together? Does your family pray together? What do you think would help you and your family become better Christians?

In asking the questions, I am prepared to record answers for myself. If I don't, it will be too easy for me to forget the responses. Taking the time to record them is evident to those with whom I am visiting that I will seriously consider their contributions.

In listening to the responses, I also try to hear beyond the words. This is where the clarification aspect comes into play. We all have words which for us have many meanings; two people can use the same word to express different ideas. Certain words have more emotional charge for some of us. So I am careful to ask for further explanations of the statements made in order to avoid misinterpretation and to facilitate the parents' own exploration of their needs, hopes, and expectations for themselves and their children.

One of the most fascinating realizations

that I made when visiting the 40 families who supposedly wanted "more structured CCD" was that these people were basically concerned about faith growth for themselves and their families. The only tradition and experience out of which they could express that concern was through that with which they were familiar, the school and CCD programs.

The question *Do you know what your children are doing in religion class?* usually spurred the discussion into a whole new realm, helping me to see that what these parents really wanted was to have an integral part in their children's religious growth. They wanted to know what their children were experiencing. They wanted to do something at home that would support those experiences but they found it difficult to know how or what to do. At this point, I began clarifying terms with them, and affirming their desires.

These parents were really saying that they wanted their children to grow (parents have always wanted that), and they wanted to provide beneficial opportunities for that growth, but they were doubting the actual power they had in effecting that growth and faith development. The answer to the dilemma for them seemed to be to strengthen that with which they were familiar, namely, the CCD program. I presented the rationale behind family catechesis, pointing out the existing situation in Christian education (as *per* Chapter 1), and indicating some of the possibilities open to families, given a change in those situations.

My experience attests that the majority of concerned Christian parents are in a similar quandry. This is in great part the fault of parish leadership which has preached the importance of parents and family in faith development, and concurrently developed elaborate programs of childhood catechesis, indirectly saying that parents are unable to guide their children's religious development. At the same time, they offer very little if anything for adult religious development.

I was once asked to give a reaction to a talk on family religious education in which the speaker placed too much emphasis on teaching religion and teaching children. Conse-

quently, in my reaction, I stressed the importance of adult catechesis as an integral aspect of family development and cautioned against making the same errors we have made in the past. After the talk, a number of parents stopped me to say: "Thank you, Sister, I'm so tired of feeling like a second-class citizen in the Church because all the time and money is put into children."

Perhaps we have told parents long enough that they are the primary and best teachers of their children. They now believe us, and we had better literally put our money and efforts behind our words. Our challenge is to enable parents to be even more powerful, effective and knowledgeable about how they can be the first, most important and best religious developers of their children, and do even better what they have been doing all along. In short, our role as ministers is to help parents to be successful parents, successful in the sense that Hubert Humphrey defined success—in that "we help develop self-esteem in someone who didn't have it before."

Often parents are slow to become involved in family programs because they simply do not believe that they can be successful transmitters of the faith simply by living that faith and being confident in what they believe and why. Our mouths have been telling them they can, while our programming and budgeting have been telling them they cannot. When I have openly stated this situation to the parents with whom I am visiting, they have given both nonverbal as well as verbal assent, which will usually be followed by very specific questions about how such a program of family catechesis would be structured.

This is the opportunity, then, to enable families to begin assuming shared responsibility of the concept and the particular program that will be established in the parish. I turn the question back to them with, "What would you see as a viable structure for your family, given your other interests and commitments?" Thus, during the course of my assessing needs, the program also begins to take shape.

Handling the assessment of needs through the informal conversation method accomplishes more than one objective. At the same time that needs are surfaced, interest in family catechesis is generated. Most of all, ideas and attitudes are clarified. Failure to clarify terms with people can bring serious bouts of depression and frustration, something neither parents nor parish staffs need.

The staff at St. Joseph's were feeling that they had failed in preparing parishioners for family catechesis when I arrived, and families

vince them that it was the best thing for them since sliced bread. They were unimpressed.

2. Convince the Pastoral Leadership

The next step in the development of a program is to convince the pastor and/or pastoral team of your parish of the need for family catechesis. In reality, this step does not necessar-

---

Aiding parents in their growth, affirming and supporting them in their roles as parents and transmitters of the faith is our most important task in the designing and implementing of family programs.

---

were feeling unheard by the staff, all because there was a misunderstanding in terminology. Significantly, of those 40 families on the sheet of paper I received, half of them formed the nucleus of the 35 families who were the initial group of a family program called *Project Family Life* (PFL), which is now over six years old and 150 families strong.

Certainly not every parishioner can be approached to provide input for this needs assessment if it is handled by the personal visit. It is sufficient to choose a random sampling or go to those who have expressed a strong interest in the religious development of their families. The people you meet with will feel honored at being chosen to give advice. They will most likely be as honest in sharing their needs, hopes, and desires with you as you are in seeking them out. They will feel an integral part of the planning process for their program and, in the future, will be your advocates to motivate the rest of the parish. In time, they may even become your co-leaders of the program. By all means, do not do what I did the first time I developed a family program for a parish. I did not assess needs with parishioners; I went in with a pre-conceived well-designed program and proceeded to try to con-

ily fit in the scheme chronologically. Rather, it is an essential element. I have been fortunate in both parishes in which I established family programs that the pastors recognized the need for such ministry in the parishes and were very supportive. The entire planning process and implementation of a family program assumes the pastoral leaders' support. Because family catechesis is a new concept to many parents and because it is frightening to many, the parish staff, especially the pastor, need to be in agreement about its worth, validity and necessity in today's Church. Many programs have been unnecessarily short-lived because the DRE considered family development a priority while the pastor did not. This is not to say that family catechesis cannot occur where there is no pastoral support but it is much more difficult.

I know of several places where groups of families gather, develop their own programs and struggle through the process to provide some meaningful family experiences for themselves while their pastors give them little more than an occasional critical, sideward glance. The task is difficult for those families and one which often ends in futility and frustration. Those groups tend to begin doubting themselves and often run out of ideas after a couple of years (don't we all, if we don't have someone who shares our visions, with whom to talk and share thoughts, dreams, experiences and new ideas). They inevitably give up, hoping that the good experiences they had for a few years will be lasting memories on which to look back as lived experiences which somehow made a difference in their lives. At this point in their history family programs need

---

So many families are unaware of the tremendous impact they have on one another and on their neighbors. Our task is to help them realize their power.

---

the support—morally, financially, and ideologically—of pastoral and catechetical leadership. In addition, to match the families' efforts, these self-initiated family programs need leadership which is likewise creative, visionary and determined. They need leaders who are willing to take risks and invite families to risk with them.

Selecting a Family Catechesis Director: Parishes that are earnest about family ministry will want to consider hiring a director of family catechesis or provide education and training for parishioners interested and able to assume the leadership of family catechesis. Even more importantly, they must be willing to affirm a director in other ways. The development and implementation of family programs in a parish take no small amount of time, energy, creativity, knowledge and skill.

In looking for a director who will develop family catechesis, the parish may want to consider the following criteria, which in my experience are worth taking into account. I present an ideal which may seem impossible to find; the ideal can always be modified to meet the specific needs of each parish.

Obviously, the parish will want to seek out a candidate who is convinced and knowledgeable of the concept of family and adult catechesis. The candidate should also be knowledgeable in applied theology or spirituality, education, psychological development and parenting skills. Teaching experience on all levels is important as is former catechetical experience in a parish. A background in the humanities would be most helpful.

As far as personal qualities, the candidate will prove most effective if s/he is organized, flexible, personable and outgoing. The parish will also want to select a person who is determined and persevering. So many family programs die immaturely because the average tenure of a parish DRE is two years. The new director who takes over often does not, or is not able to follow through on the momentum that has begun, if any recognizable momentum can be seen in such a short time. Consequently, a new direction is set and a new momentum begun. This process of starting over is hazardous to the health and growth of family programs.

Finally, and very importantly, that elusive quality of creativity. Few have gone before us in the field of family catechesis, successfully leaving workable models. The models that we have need to be adapted creatively to each individual situation. Every parish is different; the needs and desires of families in those parishes are different, and while there are some basic principles which may be more or less universally applicable, the final enfleshing of those principles depends on the local situation. The design of a program for a rural/resort parish of 300 families is very different from the design of a program for a middle-class suburban parish of 1600 families.

One of the first tasks of the new director therefore will be to become knowledgeable of the parish, its history, structure, catechetical background, and its economic status. All of this data figures strongly in the type of program that will be developed in the parish.

3. *Define Areas of Needs and Concerns*

The data collected in your needs assessment will determine to a great extent the model and format of the program you will design. It is out of need, concern and desire that programs are developed. If they do not meet the expressed needs of families, you will be humming to yourself in an empty building while your families look elsewhere for help and support.

If the needs assessment reveals a desire on the part of parents to get to know other families in the parish, you need to design programs that will facilitate the building of that kind of Christian community for parents. Parents who express a need for a theological update will not respond to a program which fails to offer that as part of its design. Families requesting help in communication skills, family activity suggestions, or training in particular parenting skills will expect to see evidence of these specifics in the program design or they will feel duped by the parish staff and will be hesitant about further participation in family catechesis.

Unless you plan to use the information received, you should not seek it out. Unless you are willing to listen honestly to the parishioners and their needs, the program you propose will probably fail for want of authenticity and cogency.

The data collected through the needs assessment will form the basis for the goals and objectives that are set for family catechesis in the parish. Similarly, it is important to recognize the strengths and weaknesses of your parish and honestly to try to respond to that information in creative ways. If, for example, 50% of the families in your parish are single-parent families, the goals and design of your program will be different than if the majority of families are two-parent families. A program in a highly ethnic area will not be the same as a program in a mixed-nationality parish. A parish that has a history of no adult education will need a program that is different from one in which adult education is a priority and has a successful history. A parish with a strong community spirit will need a program different than one in which there is little community spirit or in which a community spirit is being newly developed. A rural parish will call for a program different than that of an inner city or suburban parish. A parish with a school will have different needs than a parish without a

---

Through each personal contact with families, you can affirm their potential. We are, after all, family ministers, not designers of programs.

---

school. A family program in a parish which is 75% senior citizens may need to be questioned.

In short, it is important that you look not only at the information received through your talking with families, but also at the profile of your parish—its size, its historical background, its median age, its staff and their responsibilities (these may need to be rearranged), its concept of Church, of community, of religious education, of liturgy. This will be more clear when I discuss program design.

4. *Pre-evangelize.*

The next three steps—pre-evangelizing, setting goals, and designing the program—will probably be occurring simultaneously. As I mentioned earlier, the step, pre-evangelizing for family catechesis, actually began when the needs assessment began. Furthermore, it is an ongoing aspect of any family program because all of the people in a parish generally do not become ready for involvement in family catechesis at the same time.

Pre-evangelization for family catechesis consists of an introduction, preparation and education of parents for the concept. This is not nearly as difficult a task today as it was eight or ten years ago. Since then much has been said in both religious and secular circles about the need for family growth. We must remember, however, that we still have a 400-year history of the Church's emphasis on teaching children doctrine and dogma.

One of the approaches that I have found helpful in preparing parents to take the step toward family faith development is to acquaint them with the historical background which indicates that family catechesis is not all that new. Guiding parents through our catechetical history from Hebrew times to the present helps them to understand that family programming is not a new fad which DRE's are trying out but a sincere effort to revive a segment of our tradition which says a great deal about who we are as Church.

I usually go through a brief historical development which begins with an explanation of who the religious educators were in the Hebrew tradition, in the early Church or apostolic times, during the era of the growth of universities and monasteries and in the Middle Ages. I then proceed to indicate the change of emphasis during the Reformation, including the direction set by Trent, the American immigrant situation in the 18th and 19th centuries, right up to the present.

For a concise American historical perspective of family catechesis, I would recommend Dolores Curran's "In The Beginning Were the Parents" originally from her column *Talks With Parents.* Permission to reprint can be purchased for inclusion in the parish bulletin or it can also be purchased in 5 ½ X 8 ½ inch card-size to be distributed to interested parents (See Bibliography). I would also recommend her book *In the Beginning Were the Parents* in which that column is the first chapter. I distributed the column after my historical discourse described above and had a number of parents come up, waving it at me saying, "Thank you. Now I'm beginning to see that there really is something to this family business. Maybe it's not just a new fad."

The pre-evangelization process can utilize many forms and many techniques. Acquiring permission to reprint columns and articles about the concept of family catechesis for insertion in the parish bulletin is an easy approach. The authors or sources of the articles are usually honored to have you reprint their material and frequently do not charge a reprint fee.

I include a bit of information which I found most effective in helping parents realize the influence they have on their children, just in terms of sheer time spent with them. The information, computed by an associate DRE in the Minneapolis-St. Paul archdiocese, also virtually portrays the exaggerated expectations placed upon the school and religious education programs.

From the time a child is born until s/he reaches his/her fifth birthday, that child has spent 43,800 hours within the influence of the home. When that child begins school and spends 5 ½ hours daily for 180 days, s/he has spent 990 hours within the influence of the teacher and classroom peers. For the school to have the same length of time to influence the child as the home has, it would require about 44 ½ years of that child's lifetime. When a child enters a religious education program attending classes one hour per week for 21 weeks of the year, then s/he would need to be within the parish setting 2,089 ½ years to be exposed to the same amount of influence as is possible within the home setting the first five years of life.

In addition to using others' writings in your bulletin, writing your own column helps to incorporate the specific needs of your parish with the general rationale of family catechesis and makes the notion less theoretical. I did this in a four-segment bulletin insert shortly before beginning our program seven years ago. The information provided precipitated questions which enabled me to meet and talk with even more people before the program began.

A specially scheduled series of evenings for parents, sponsored in conjunction with the parish adult education program, is another forum for relaying the theory and rationale behind family catechesis. Sessions to enrich parenting skills in such areas as communication, topics of concern such as television and the family, presentations on a family approach to sacramental preparation and family prayer, courses on the stages of moral and faith development—all of these possibilities of collaborating with other parish programs and parish staff are ways to pre-evangelize for family catechesis.

I have found it most helpful to invite guest speakers who share my vision, to say some of the same things I have been saying so that parishioners realize that this is not just my own wild idea.

There are also numerous tapes, filmstrips, and films that can be useful in this step of pre-evangelizing. One of the finest that I have seen is a tape/slide presentation accompanied by a book, which comprises *Family Time: A Revolutionary Old Idea,* prepared and published by the Family Communication Committee of the Million Dollar Round Table (an Insurance Company) for the Bicentennial. Their focus is simple: "No other success can compensate for failure in the home. Each family would benefit from a weekly time together spent on quality projects, events, times that enrich, deepen and bring joy to family living." The tape/slide presentation is well done. It is highly motivational, and its accompanying little book follows up with myriad suggestions for practical projects and activities for the family to do together. Both families unfamiliar with such a concept as well as parents who have already been a part of the family program respond positively to the audio-visual segment of *Family Time.*

Since the slide presentation lasts about 15 minutes, you might consider using it at your weekend parish liturgy. The book could then be offered for sale afterwards. I do not ordinarily recommend that sort of use of the liturgy; I do so now cautiously. It is easy to fall prey to the temptation of having the "captive

audience." Whatever is said about family catechesis should be within the context of the scriptures for the day, since the homily should not be a vehicle for education but for breaking open the Word, so that it might inspire and challenge us toward Christian action. The Feast of the Holy Family, for example, would be an appropriate occasion to use the *Family Time* slide/audio presentation.

Some caution also about terminology during this period of pre-evangelization: In order

Parish leadership has preached the importance of parents and family in faith development, and concurrently developed elaborate programs of childhood catechesis, indirectly saying that parents are unable to guide their children's religious development.

to help parents become comfortable and at ease with the concept of family catechesis, we need to refrain from heavy phrases such as: "Parents are teachers of religion," and "It is the duty of parents to teach their children religion." Such statements are not only frightening to parents but are also untrue and misleading. I refer back to the definition of family catechesis: the main goal in developing family programs is to strengthen and affirm parents in their rightful role as *mediators of the faith* not as teachers of some subject in a classroom.

I recommend that you speak of parents sharing faith, values, and attitudes with their children, and speak of it as their right which no one ought take from them. Help them to see that the Church is offering them an opportunity to grow in faith with their families and with their parish community. Aid them in understanding faith as an act of the person in an affective relationship, and thereby enable them to realize that even in the most simple activities we engage in we are sharing Christianity with our children. Appeal to the natural question; "What's in it for me?" Then lead them beyond that level of interest.

One of the ways that I responded to that query is to tell parents that involvement in the family program means they don't have to feel guilty when the request for CCD teachers is made because they have chosen to share their faith through another structure for a time. I have also pointed out that the program will help them develop skills that they need to accomplish their hopes and dreams for their children.

At first, you might appeal to the parents on the basis of what the program will provide for their children, but before long they realize through their own experiences in the program that it is their own growth in faith that most effectively nurtures their children's growth.

As the program ages, you will no longer have to do the bulk of motivating. Those who have experienced the program will do it for you. The summer after our first year of Project Family Life, as a means of recruiting families for the program, I asked couples who had been part of the program to invite three or four other couples into their homes for informal get-togethers. I also was present and used a short tape on the concept of family catechesis. Then I just spent time talking a bit and answering questions. During the course of the evening in almost every situation, the host couple took over to answer the questions out of their own experience since spending a year in the program. And I simply listened.

Another year, we invited couples to speak from the pulpit (after Communion) about their experiences in the program. During those two years the program tripled and doubled. Word also will spread without a planned forum if the program is effectively meeting family needs. The last two years I did not formally publicize the program except to produce a brochure which included the aim, rationale and structure of the program and some quotes from families who had participated. The program still grew, though not as radically as those first years.

Care should be taken in this process, however, to prepare your people and publicize your program without over-sell. One of the initial mistakes we made at St. Joseph was to over-sell. This happened naturally out of our enthusiasm and commitment to the concept and the program. But I suspect that our program would probably have involved even more families if we hadn't pushed it so hard. Of course, seven years ago we were also using phrases such as "parents are teachers," and once a phrase is used long and often enough, the damage is difficult to undo. In any event, over-publicizing could be detrimental to a program. Such a technique sometimes makes

---

One of my goals is to integrate family faith development with the larger parish community's expression of its faith.

---

people skeptical. They begin to wonder, if it is so good, why does it have to be advertised so forcefully?

One of the most effective methods of preparing families for family catechesis is to offer family experiences which demonstrate what is being written and talked about in the parish. These do not have to be long-termed or complex. They are simple opportunities through which families can experience sharing faith in a nonthreatening, enjoyable manner—something, for example, planned around a liturgical or natural season—something which incorporates a sense of community spirit as well as family spirit.

Since most of planning for fall takes place in the spring, and since fall will probably be the time when most parishes would incorporate a new program, why not whet families' appetites with a "Family Welcoming of Spring." This would obviously be tied in with the beginning of the Lenten season. It could begin the way we usually end parties, with cake, ice cream, balloons, games, etc. for an intense 45 minutes, with the constant encouragement to eat everything that is present and do as much in that short time as possible. Then follow with time during which the people are asked to let the air out of the balloons and clean up the area as quietly as possible, again in a short amount of time, about ten minutes at the most.

Those tasks completed, tell the story of the origin of Lent, in your own words, including the following ideas: *Lent and springtime are in a very real sense synonymous. Both are times when life struggles for triumph over*

and other perishables.

Our word **carnival** *originally applied to this end-of-winter party; it means "getting rid of the meat." Mardi Gras, or Fat Tuesday, as it is sometimes called, is a continuation of this end-of-winter party. With the meat and other perishables consumed, however, there were some weeks of rather low rations for people until animals came out of hibernation and the new crops were grown.*

People in the early Church lived this way. And so, in the centuries when the faith was spreading across Europe and mixing with other religions, the natural penance and fasting of springtime became the Lent of the Church. It became a time when public sinners sat in sackcloth and ashes doing penance for their sins, and a time of renewal and re-initiation for everyone else. While life in nature struggled to get the upper hand over the death-likeness of winter, Christians struggled with the evil within them through fasting, praying and penance, to enable a new life of conversion to spring forth. Lent is still such a time for us.

The story could be followed by some scripture, perhaps Paul's exhortation to "get rid of the old person and put on the new," some

---

We achieve the goal of integration of family catechesis into the total life of the parish not through instruction about the concept but through immersion of families into the total life experience of the parish.

---

death. The practices of Lent are about as old as spring itself. Years ago, before refrigerators, freezers and grocery stores, people's lives were dictated by the climate. The end of winter meant a scarcity of provisions. The last of the meat frozen in a snowbank or salted was in danger of spoiling with the arrival of occasional warm days. Rather than that happening, people held a festival to consume at one happy time all that was left of the meat

discussion of its meaning for us, and then an invitation to parents to share with their own families what Lent was like for them as children. Families could also be asked to make a family resolution for Lent and perhaps even take some time to determine individual resolutions to aid their lenten growth. A ritual for an Ash Wednesday service at home could be passed out, and the day could close with prayer. The whole experience takes perhaps two hours; there is some follow-up for families at home and the program leaves a pleasant taste of what family catechesis is about. If you have the time and personnel, *Ashes to Easter* and *Major Feasts and Seasons* (Volume 1, number 2) have suggestions for Lenten neighborhood gatherings which can be easily adapted for your group of families.

5. Set Goals and Objectives

Goals and objectives grow out of needs, concerns and future hopes. They put theories into workable, organized formats for implementation. They are future-oriented blueprints for action. If, in your needs assessment, you found that parents were asking to be updated in theology, then you will want a goal which speaks to adult theological development. If families indicated a desire to know how to tell their children about various aspects of the faith, then you will want a goal which states that parents will be aided in communicating faith to their children. If parents in your parish feel the need for support of a community or for simple parenting skills, then your goals will be formed around those needs. Once formulated, it will be important to prioritize them. Decisions will have to be made with regard to the importance of each goal, and some have to be met before others.

In looking at the previous examples, it is probably necessary to deal with the development of a support community and parenting skills before attempting the theological growth, and to introduce basic communication skills in preparation for communicating from the depths of their faith. Each parish will have different needs and therefore different goals, and consequently, no one program model will work equally well in all parishes.

Goals for family programs ought also be aimed toward the future *three* to *five* years hence, with specific step-by-step objectives to help achieve those goals. Family programs, if they are to be effective, should be long-range and developmental. They are concerned with the growth and development of families within the Christian community and therefore

need to grow with families. The token six-week family program that is planned for Lent because "we should do something family" lacks a sense of commitment to the concept of family ministry in the parish. The short-term effort toward family catechesis, if done well, can become a powerful catalyst for the further development of the concept, but it should be designed with that purpose in mind. It is used as an *hors d'oeuvre* which is followed by the rest of the meal.

Years ago, I set down five general goals which were long-range and developmental. I share them with you with some explanations, because having worked for me, they may be helpful to you.

1. To realize that the family is a unique community in itself and that the quality of its life has implications which extend beyond the home.
2. To return the Christian growth and formation of children to its proper realm i.e., the home.
3. To give adults of the community an opportunity to develop a more sound understanding of Christianity today. To educate and update them in theology, communication and other parenting skills so that they are comfortable in sharing their faith, values and religion with their families.
4. To help place the institutional Church, its clergy and Religious in their proper perspective, i.e., as leaders and guides of the Christian Community in contrast to teachers of children.
5. To integrate family faith development with the larger parish community's expression of its faith.

In my visits with parents, I became aware of the need to support and affirm them in their role as communicators of the faith. They already believed that the religious development of their children was their right but they wanted help to be able to facilitate that development more effectively. They also needed to be encouraged to believe in themselves and in what they were already doing. St. Joseph's had, and still has a highly intelligent, skilled, creative and powerful staff. While parents believed what the staff was telling them about their rightful responsibility to their children, they were at the same time rather intimidated by the staff's abilities and tended to relinquish their children to the staff and their programs rather than attempt family experiences. Similarly, they were not aware of the numerous family experiences through which they were already transmitting their religious faith and values. Thus, goals 1, 2, and 4 emerged.

Parents also expressed a desire to learn "what the Church really believed" since Vatican II, so that they could communicate sound Christianity to their children. Few, if any, wanted to subject their children to what they had been subjected. They had had sufficient opportunities for a good introduction to the theological updating of the late 60's and early 70's to want to be even more informed. At the same time, they wanted their children to learn that theology in a systematic way, since that was their only experience of religious training.

Learning this information precipitated goal 3 with an objective to help parents understand some of the basics behind how and when children learn and how faith and morality develop in people. It also meant that since parents were committing themselves to risk family catechesis, there had to be evidence of a developmental planning in the program that would meet the needs of people at various stages of development. It meant that I should have encouraged only families with young children (babies to 10 or 11 years old) to join the program, so that the program could develop with them. I didn't, and as a result, we had a few years of trying to provide something for everyone. That was difficult.

I strongly suggest that you design your program for young families at first. It is easier for parents to begin family activities and rituals at home when the children are younger. Parents are going to feel strange and uncomfortable at first, with some of the activities, and having older children who are feeling the same is not helpful to them. In fact, the natural inclina-

tion is not to try. As those families grow in age, other structures can be built into the program to meet the needs of families of older children. I have found that both the children and the parents in families who have a tradition of family catechesis want to continue in

---

Parish programs need not compete, but rather provide options. And where there are options, there can be real choice.

---

that vein even as the children move into the junior and senior high age levels, but that requires a somewhat different structural approach. In a future chapter, I will describe in more detail how that might be done, and some of the ways in which we tried to accomplish it.

The goal to integrate family catechesis into the total parish ministry may at first be difficult, but it should definitely be within the long-range plan for the program. The goal can be achieved at least occasionally by developing a program around the actions and rituals of the parish community and broader Christian community.

I began by working from a general theme each year. The themes were determined and developed in such a way that one built upon the other. For the first year of the program, our theme was the *Liturgical Year,* chosen for two reasons. First, parents had told me during my needs assessment that they really wanted to do things at home with their children which would help them communicate their faith with their children. One of the easiest ways to initiate family religious activities is to capitalize on the holidays—Christmas, Advent, Lent, Easter, Thanksgiving, etc. Secondly, adults who have celebrated these seasons year

A community of believers is created only when the adults in that community realize that being Christian requires freely accepting and choosing to witness Christ.

after year for some 30 or 40 years, welcome the opportunity to pause and examine what it is that we are really celebrating and ritualizing.

So the use of the liturgical theme accomplished several of my goals, at least in part. It helped educate and update parents theologically. It returned some important religious development to the family. It helped enact the fact that the family is a unique community and the quality of its life has implications beyond itself, since many of the activities that were performed at home promoted a renewed kind of celebration of those seasonal rituals at church, and in some cases, promoted the extension of the nuclear family's activities toward the broader Christian community. As time went on, families were encouraged to invite other families to join in some of their rituals and activities. Lent especially provided opportunities for families to reach out to others, through the activities of our parish Social Action Center.

We accomplish the goal of integration of family catechesis into the total life of the parish not through instruction about the concept but through immersion of families into the total faith life experience of the parish. That means that in designing a family program, we must look carefully at the total parish. The improvement of the quality of family faith life in the parish will have to have the support of a quality parish faith life in which to be integrated. At the same time, as the quality of

family life improves, so will the quality of parish life. The two affect each other simultaneously. Growing families will not remain in a parish that shows no evidence of a community spirit, that celebrates liturgies like the turning of a prayer wheel, that has little pastoral concern for people, and has little or no involvement in social justice.

Seeing the totality of parish ministry subdivided into five categories, each of which is necessary to the other, was helpful to our parish. The credit for this rightfully goes to the total staff at St. Joseph's. It began to fall together for us after many hours of theologizing, discussing, arguing and studying our parish situation. The credit for the diagram, which finally made our struggles and conclusions visible and clear to us goes to the pastor, Blaine Barr, who probably understood it all long before it became clear to the rest of us.

The five basic ministries are: Liturgical Ministry (Worship and Prayer), Catechetical Ministry (Preaching and Teaching the Word), Social Ministry (Social Services and Social Action), Pastoral Ministry (Pastoral Care, Counseling, Healing), and the Ministry of Building Christian Community (developing the environment in which faith is nurtured and grows).

None of these can exist without the others and the absence of one diminishes the effectiveness of the others. It is impossible to have meaningful liturgical prayer without a sense of community spirit; likewise, it is impossible to worship without some understanding of the meaning of the Word in our lives. Making the Word present in our lives similarly enhances our prayer lives, and honest living of the Word. Lives of prayer naturally challenge and lead us to respond in healing love and service with other Christians who believe and love with us.

Furthermore, the circle is not closed to the parish community only, but the growth experienced within the parish naturally directs us outward to the broader world community, and the growth experienced outside the parish is brought back with us and shared within the parish community. Understanding catechesis

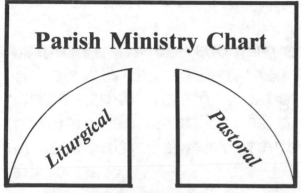

Parish Ministry Chart

Liturgical

Pastoral

Ministry of
Building Christian Community

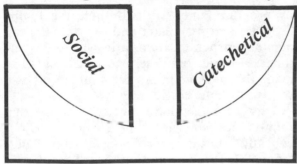

Social

Catechetical

as a pastoral activity which includes not just education, but integration of persons into the totality of Christian life, helps us in the designing and developing of family programs which are means whereby total families can experience the conscious and active faith life of persons and of a Christian community.

It strikes me that it is precisely to this type of integration, that the authors of the pastoral message *To Teach As Jesus Did* were referring when they charged educators to direct their educational efforts around the message, the community experience, and service. To these, I would add incorporation into the ritual life of people and of the community. Catechesis is always much more than just the imparting of the message. Proclaiming the Good News utilizes more than just the mouth. To really proclaim is to speak, act, dance, skip, stoop to help, reach to accept, and be silent to watch and pray.

Two final comments about goals and objectives of family programs. It is important to

develop objectives which equally promote both individual family activities and activities with groups of families. The group sessions that you have with adults and families ought to stimulate similar activities to happen in the home.

It is likewise important to stress equally those activities which promote their life as family and their faith life as Christian family.

In this age of homage to the goal and objective, it is easy to become mired in the composition of goals for your program. But behind them all is one simple task—to empower families. Through each personal contact with families, you can affirm their potential. We are, after all, family ministers, not designers of programs.

So many families are unaware of the tremendous impact they have on one another and on their neighbors. Our task is to help them realize their power. Rosemary Haughton expressed the ministerial power of families so beautifully in her working paper presented at the American Bishops Bicentennial hearings in Atlanta, Georgia on August 9, 1975. In referring to a seldom referred to passage in the Vatican II Decree on the *Apostolate of the Laity* (Chapter 3, section 11) she says:

"*. . . there is an almost prophetic quality about that passage from the Council's document which firmly, almost ruthlessly, sets the Christian family at the heart of the Church's mission of compassion for the world which God loves so much.*

"*That, then, is the vocation of the family in the Church—to discover its identity, to fulfill its needs, to grow in unity and loyalty by responding—each in its own way—to the Christian vocation of loving service.*

"*. . . Families, just because they have a continuous, ordinary, everyday life of their own and don't exist* just *to provide help, can give the sense of belonging, a feeling of positive, future-facing life.*

"*But if the Church demands all this of the Christian family—and it can and it does and it must for the sake of the family and of those they serve—what can the Church do for these*

When children enter a religious education program attending classes one hour per week for 21 weeks of the year, then they would need to be within the parish setting 2,089 ½ years to be exposed to the same amount of influence as is possible within the home setting the first five years of life.

families? I suggest that the Church can do what it has formerly done for those engaged in special and demanding work for God. The Church can give them recognition. It can officially and explicitly support them, proclaiming their status as people called to serve in important ways.''

Finally, as you reach the point of setting down goals and objectives and determining a program design, incorporate parents into the process. They know what their schedules are, what they will feel comfortable participating in and what they would not feel comfortable with. They will know what their children, and what they, too, will respond to and what will not be inviting to them. They usually have a better understanding of family life than those of us who live celibate life styles or who are committed to full-time Church work. (Married or not, DRE's share the occupational hazard of being unrealistic when it comes to family programming.) Inviting parents who are interested in a program for themselves and the rest of the parish will help to keep us honest, and at least within the realms of plausibility.

Another word of caution before proceeding to program design: I do not recommend at this time in our history, that a family program in a parish replace other catechetical programs that are already existing in the parish. I have seen several parishes discontinue all elementary religious education in favor of a fam-ily program, only to discontinue the family program two years later and reinstate the elementary program, reinstating at the same time, all the errors described in Chapter 1. I made this mistake in my youthful enthusiasm for family catechesis.

This recommendation is not to imply that family programs are experimental religious education, but it is to recognize that a change from 400 years of tradition takes time. Nor is it to imply that a critical look at other parish programs is not in order and that some of them might need re-designing. For example, I am not at all sure that most CCD classes are in keeping with valid catechetical principles, nor in keeping with what is best for children. It is to recognize that no single program will meet everyone's needs. Parish programs need not compete, but rather they provide options. And where there are options, there can be real choice.

6. *Design The Program.*

After determining the needs of families in the parish and formulating the goals for family catechesis, we come to the critical step of designing the program itself. At this point we often make our biggest mistake: go out and buy a published program or use a model from another parish, almost disregarding the findings of our own situation. I have reservations about published programs, only because the programs that I have seen work best are those that come out of the creativity of the people involved and are custom designed for a particular group of people at a particular time. These programs are also the ones that are the most flexible and most developmental. They grow and change with the people who are a part of them.

There are five basic models of family programs in use around the country today. Many others are combinations of these five. A description of these five, with advantages and disadvantages of each, as I see them, may be helpful in your designing a program for your parish.

Peer Group Centered: The most common example and probably the most widely used of the peer-centered models is the Paulist Press Family Program. This model brings the total family together at the same time for educational input, and then separates them according to age or grade level for an hour of class time. The various groups are brought together again before the end of the evening for some group or family activities related to the topic all have been studying. Parishes which use this model most often end the session with the celebration of the Eucharist.

The model was initially designed for rural areas and it does work well in such an environment. In fact, it works well in various environments as is attested by its popularity. I used a similar model in a rural area, but am now aware of numerous opportunities for family growth in that environment which I allowed to slip by at the time because I was caught up in my own structure. I will share some possibilities for various sizes and locations of parishes later.

The advantages of the peer group or Paulist model are that it enables the total family to come for catechesis at the same time and to concentrate on the same topic. This can be especially beneficial for further sharing at home. It is a good transition from the CCD model, since it is basically a CCD model anyway with the addition of classes for parents and the opportunity for all the classes to be going on at the same time, thus requiring only one trip to the church per month or twice a month for religious education for each family.

Another value in this model is that adult education is an integral part of the structure. Parents must attend if their children are to attend. It is also developmental in its approach to themes and topics, though some of the topics are repetitious from year to year, and a few are decidedly abstruse; the development of them for children becomes dangerously oversimplified. The model can be fairly easily integrated into the total life of the parish, depending on what is done with each topic.

There certainly are possibilities for providing opportunities for families to live out the information given at the class sessions within the parish community between meetings, since most parishes using this model meet monthly. Such integration of the program into other aspects of parish life may take a little more time and creativity, and the potential is one which allows you to supplement the program with additional intergenerational experiences.

The advantage of a parish choosing to use the already developed Paulist Family Program is having the basic research, lesson plans, slides, tapes, handouts, etc. done for you. The slides, incidentally, are very good, and for the most part, so are the scripts that go with them. There is, however, also a disadvantage to this seeming benefit, a disadvantage that I have seen destroy family programs repeatedly. The program was obviously designed to be used as a tool and to be modified as necessary for individual utilization. Unfortunately, it becomes just too easy to match the code numbers out of the kit, skim the contents quickly, make the copies needed and hope for the best. Before long, the program no longer meets the needs for which family catechesis was initiated, families drop out and we assume family catechesis doesn't work and store the substantial investment we made in a dark closet somewhere.

The substantial cost of the program I see as another disadvantage, particularly when you consider that a fair amount of time will be spent after buying the program making the changes necessary for your particular situation.

I also think the program is more expensive than it is worth considering the additional redesigning that may be necessary on a local level. I am waiting for Paulist to sell the slides and scripts for some of their sessions separately. They would be worth my money, since

the sessions, and it does not really offer much time for real family or intergenerational faith sharing.

While the peer group model may be a good way to begin a family approach to catechetics, the model should not be clung to, but be innovatively remodeled as soon as families are ready to move from that form of traditional educational model.

The improvement of the quality of family faith life in the parish will have to have the support of a quality parish faith life in which to be integrated.

---

they are well done, and not as easily accessible as lesson plan ideas and take-home suggestions for various topics.

The organization of the program's many components is fairly complex. I ordered one of the cycles for examination when they were first published and sent it back after two days. It took me that long to figure out the code and put all of the material together for one session, and that didn't include the time I would have put into modification of the material. Granted, I personally find it easier to start from scratch on a topic and create it myself than to put that type of puzzle together.

The greatest disadvantage I see in this model is that it is not really a family model, but an extended CCD model, which makes some of the same mistakes that we are already making—namely, assuming that religion is something to be learned as facts in an instructional setting. The difference in this case is that this kind of learning is attempted by everyone in the family at the same time. Unfortunately, those parents who are involved in the teaching of the various groups are unable to be an integral part of the total program. It still places too much emphasis on the teaching of religion to children, beginning with four-and five-year-olds who are in a separate group during

The program at St. Joseph's parish began as a model similar to this one, but was changed within a year and a half at the request of the parents. I shall explain that transformation later. Interestingly, the Paulist program was initially designed to be simply a catalyst for further development on the local level. Paulist has since published cycles four and five which indicates that the program has become another form of textbook rather than a means of inspiration for creative development in parishes.

Family Learning Teams: This model is designed around the educational concept of open classroom learning centers. Joseph and Mercedes Iannone who piloted the model originally at Good Shepherd Parish in Alexandria, Virginia, are most often credited for its design and development and conduct training sessions through the National Training Center for Family Learning Teams. However, Locke Bowman, a Protestant educator who has Intergenerational Learning Centers in Scottsdale, Arizona has done some valuable work in the field and is not as well known in Catholic circles.

Family Learning Teams consist of groups of approximately 15 families within a particular neighborhood who assume responsibility for the religious education of one another in that particular geographic area. Every adult performs some task for the religious education of those families, for example, providing hospitality, teaching, making cookies, planning liturgies or neighborhood picnics etc. The families then meet together on a regular basis for learning and activities. Depending

hood discussions with other adults

Unfortunately, this model also can easily become child-centered, since its basic premise is that the adults assume the responsibility for religious education of the neighborhood children. The learning center activities are often designed for children, the emphasis is again on learning, and parents tend to participate because it is good for their children and out of

---

At the same time as the quality of family life improves, so will the quality of parish life. The two affect each other simultaneously.

---

on need, the groups deal more or less with doctrine, and the neighborhood activities play a large part in the program structure. In some cases, the groups of families meet in homes; in other situations, the Learning Team centers are set up at the parish center, and families come in to participate at the learning centers of their choice.

In areas where the Learning Teams meet within the neighborhood, this model provides for community building. Families get to know one another and, in a very real sense, minister to one another through their involvement in the program. Likewise, where the teams gather in one another's homes, parents assume responsibility for the religious education of not only their own children, but also the children of their neighborhood.

The neighborhood model makes possible the involvement of several age groups including Senior Citizens, as well as single people in many of the activities to provide an intergenerational experience. The training for adults who are providing the leadership in this model provides opportunity for some adult education. Further, it motivates these adults to avail themselves of further opportunities and materials and to engage in some good neighbor-

a sense of responsibility to one another's children.

If families in your parish indicated a priority of interest in getting to know and share with other families in the parish, this is a good model with which to begin. Similarly, if yours is a large parish, the neighborhood grouping could be used to facilitate building a sense of community. And finally, if your needs assessment revealed a wide spectrum of interests and concerns, the learning center idea could help meet that plurality of needs. It can provide several options for families at a given time, at a central location. The organization involved in such a model, however, is immense and may very well consume most of your time.

Family Clusters: Designed and introduced by Margaret Sawin, the Family Clusters model is structured around groups of four to five families, or about 25 people, gathering together for a period of approximately six weeks at a time. Families tend to get to know one another well in this model, often becoming lasting friends. If families can be grouped for clustering according to geographic proximity, this model can facilitate community building on a neighborhood level, particularly in a large parish. If the parish is small enough, the community building becomes a natural outgrowth of the cluster model, especially as families feel comfortable enough to move from one cluster group to another.

People who choose to participate in clusters are asked to sign a contract to stay with the group for the duration of the session. This provides for commitment to the program and

---

The goal to integrate family catechesis into the total parish ministry may be difficult at first, but it should definitely be within the long range plan for the program.

---

eliminates early dropout and absenteeism which can be a problem in other models.

Those who choose this model must take special care to see that its six-week modules are related developmentally. Neither is adult education an integral part of the model, which in my opinion, is a necessary aspect of family growth. I find, too, that many of the activities used in clustering are what I call "gamey," or what a friend of mine refers to as "Walt Disney Religion." As a result, they get tiring for the adults and the adolescents, who eventually might prefer a "National Geographic approach," as it were.

In spite of these vulnerable areas, and especially with cognizance of them, the cluster model has tremendous possibilities as a basic model for at least a part of the parish family program, or as an additional family program model in a large parish. At St. Joseph's we have both Project Family Life and Family Clusters as possible family program models for people.

Liturgy Model: This is a model that is fairly prevalent in parishes because it is convenient. It is implemented in various ways, the most common being to bring families together for Sunday Liturgy, divide them into peer grouping and spend about an hour studying the readings for the day or some particular readings chosen for that day. This study time is considered the Liturgy of the Word. That completed, the groups come back together to go quickly through the Liturgy of the Eucharist and be on their way, or possibly to share coffee and donuts afterward. A second arrangement is to celebrate the Eucharist without a homily, and then move into peer groups for an hour of education.

I see no advantage in this model. Frankly, I do not see it as a valid model of family catechesis. It is a misuse of the Liturgy as well as a poor understanding of catechesis. The Liturgy is not a method of education. The Liturgy is the time when the community gathers to worship. The community comes together to remember and solemnize its lived experiences, to spend time with the Lord, to complete what is already in process, and as John Shea says, to tell the story and break the bread. It is not a time to be educated but to experience our lives and the Lord's presence to us.

By adding an educational goal to our Eucharistic worship, we do a disservice to both our worship and our educational ministries in the parish and accomplish the goals of neither ministry very well. I know of one parish in particular that has used this model for a number of years with some unfortunate results. Their parish has become split between the family program community and the rest of the community. The family community has become an elitist group in the eyes of the rest of the community. This seems decidedly contrary to the nature of Christian community.

Sacramental Hopscotching: Another model which has little validity as a paradigm of family programming is the model of Family Sacramental Preparations. The coining of the term "Sacramental Hopscotching" is credited to the creativity of Dolores Curran. I think the term captures exactly what this model is. It usually begins with a notice in the parish bulletin which goes something like: ''It is a parish policy that all parents take the Eucharist (Penance, Baptism, Confirmation) preparation course with their children before their children can receive that sacrament.'' And so, the parish claims to have family catechesis because it has a two-week preparation course for Baptism, a seven-week preparation course for Eucharist, a six-week preparation course for Reconciliation and a four-week preparation course for Confirmation, all of which are more or less effective depending on the content, development and implementation of the program.

In the eyes of many people, this inclusion of parents in the religious education of children is considered a response to a teachable moment. The question is, is it really a teachable moment and if so, for whom? Often it is more a forced situation rather than a response to an inquiry that arises spontaneously. Teachable moments occur before, during and after the event of the course or the reception of the sacrament. Furthermore, teachable moments do not center only around sacraments. Using the term to refer to those times which are most opportune for the parish to bring families together for family catechesis is a misuse of the concept.

Involving parents in the sacramental preparation of their children was in many ways the entrance to family catechesis. It evidences a tremendous catechetical potential and can serve as an initiation into further participation in family catechesis for some people. A family sacramental program can even be the initial step in the further development of a program in a parish. It can serve as a form of pre-evangelization for what family catechesis is about. It cannot, however, be an excuse for family catechesis in a parish, even though large numbers of parishes claim to have family programs because they provide sacramental preparation courses for the family while at the same time demanding attendance at them so that the reception of the sacrament becomes a sort of reward at the end of the course.

The important thing to remember about developing a model for family catechesis in the parish is that no one of the above models is necessarily the total answer for any one parish. The value of the models is in the creative ideas they can generate for you in your particular situation. One or more of the various aspects of them may be useful in view of your particular needs. What is important to re-

---

As the family-centered program ages, you will no longer have to do the bulk of motivating. Those who have experienced the program will do it for you.

---

member is that your program must meet your needs and the best program for your parish will come from you and your parishioners, and not out of a box or a training session or a sheaf of papers—not even out of this book, though hopefully here you will be able to obtain some seeds of ideas that can spread, grow and ripen into something of value for you.

Above all, in planning and designing a program, look toward something long-term, ongoing and developmental. Include for parents an integration of parenting skills, communication skills, theology, support and affirmation for what they are already doing in their families, and opportunities for them to share those family experiences with one another. That seems like a great deal, but that is indeed what being a director of family catechesis is all about. If we are going to help parents, we have to try exceptionally hard to put ourselves in the situations of parents. Making yourself available to the ''table ministry'' I referred to in the needs assessment section can be a tremendous help in doing that, if you are among those of us who are not of the family vocation.

Once you have shared food with a family you not only have an entirely different relationship with that total family, you also have some insight into what it is to be a member of that family, and of families in general. You have shared faith as well as bread with them, and they with you. You have come to know the children and they you, you have become more real in their eyes. I have a totally different relationship with families in the parish with whom I have shared a meal than with those with whom I have not. A significant amount of your time definitely should be spent in that kind of family ministry if you hope to have a successful and effective family program. It cannot all come from your head and desk; much of it will have to come from your heart and personality and personal contact with individual families in the program. It

---

Family catechesis is essentially adult centered and its focus is the sharing of faith rather than doctrine.

---

is not the program structure or model that makes family catechesis effective; it is the *people* who implement the program who make it effective.

In designing and implementing your program, beware of child-centeredness and "cute" experiences. Some "Walt-Disney faith sharing" is advisable but there also comes a time for the "National Geographic" approach. I have found that using ritual is one of the best ways to incorporate both ap-

proaches and reach total families best.

Above all, in your programming, stress the teachable moment. I find that there never can be enough emphasis on that for parents. Through emphasis on the teachable moment, we can provide some of the strongest support and affirmation for what is already being done in families. Provide suggestions for family rituals and activities which can initiate teachable moments in the home. These can often be suggestions for parents to use at home to prepare the family for the experiences that will take place in the parish. Remember always that the family program structure that takes place at the parish is only a stimulus and impetus for what actually takes place within and outside the family.

Our family catechesis bears its fruit away from us, not in front of us. Very often the only way we are able to know if what we are doing has any effect is if families are willing to share their experiences and reflection on those experiences with us.

Finally, try diligently to integrate your program into the total life of your parish, into the worship, the healing, the social action, the community building. Have it as a constant concern in your mind as you implement your program. I will give some specific examples of how this can happen in a future chapter. Remember, the parish's greatest contribution to family is through the support, encouragement, and affirmation it gives to parents. Whatever you do to help parents experience success in their role as parents and mediators of faith, values and attitudes, you do for the families in your parish.

7. *Implement the program*

You are now ready to begin the implementation of your program. I would like to share some of the developmental process of *Project Family Life* to help demonstrate how this can be done, with some suggestions for innovations in parishes other than in a suburban setting where PFL makes its home.

Chapter 3

We Call It Piffle

A Case Study of a Parish Family Program

Project Family Life was officially born and christened on a hot, early August afternoon in 1973. Four of us—Jim, our adult education director; Dean, director of senior high religious education; Mike, our liturgist; and I— met in my office for a Coke break. Before long, I was expounding on the aim, rationale, structure and possible first year theme of the proposed family-centered program for St. Joseph's parish. I was finished with most of my needs-assessment visiting which I began in June, and after some weeks of thinking and mentally experimenting with various model ideas based on the needs and concerns expressed, had completed a first draft of the program.

The Coke break was actually a comfortable setting arranged to get some feedback on the proposed draft from my team members. I had met with each of them periodically during the summer to share my findings and their expertise, but this time I was ready to share a total picture with them. One of the greatest advantages in designing a family program is having team members who support you and are willing to help plan and share their talents and experience with you. These three men were invaluable to me during those planning stages. Each added his own expertise. All had worked at St. Joseph's for a year or more, so their knowledge of the parish was particularly helpful.

As our discussion neared its end, and this new addition to the parish's educational structure began to take on a shape with which I thought parishioners would be comfortable, I said, "But it has to have a name." (I'm one of those people who names not only her pet poodle, but her car, her plants, and even her furniture arrangements.) Several trite names were tossed about, then some terribly intellectual ones, not a few cynical suggestions surfaced, and then finally, Jim presented a piece of paper on which he was doodling, bearing the words: PROJECT: FAMILY LIFE IN FAITH ENRICHMENT = PROJECT FAMILY LIFE. I liked it immediately.

The name expressed the essence of my rationale. I knew it was right. It said nothing about education and a great deal about family life and family growth and development in faith. Jim pointed out further that it could be shortened to just its initials, PFL. Having a penchant for acronyms, I retorted, "Right, and we can call it piffle." And so PFL was born and christened with Coke and three godfathers.

What's in a name? It has been said that people live up to their names, and there was some concern that the program might be considered inconsequential with a name like Piffle, so we agreed that we would use *Project Family Life,* or just the initials PFL. But somehow, that didn't last, and before long, Project Family Life was affectionately dubbed *Piffle* by participants, staff and all but the most sophisticated people. Our fears over the name indicating an insignificance of the program were unwarranted; instead, the acronym gave the program a feeling of homeyness, commonness, familiarity and spontaneity. Children liked saying the word, and even the very young were able to pronounce it. In hindsight, I think the name kept the program from becoming staid, prosaic, artificial, or sophisticated—none of which is the average family condition—something that can easily happen to catechetical programs.

PFL has its ups and downs, but in general, manages to be a program in which families can feel a comfort level that is in keeping with their lifestyle. Of course, not all the credit for that can go to the name. Participants set the tenor of a program, and the people of St. Joseph's are neither staid, prosaic, artificial nor sophisticated, and neither is the "Piffle Lady," as I soon came to be known.

St. Joseph's is a parish that is both 102 years old and 12 years old. It is one of those parishes that mushroomed with the development of additional Minneapolis suburbs in the 60's. Initially a small rural parish of not more than 200 households, a rearrangement of parish boundaries and the appointment of a new pastor in 1967 made the parish a community of 800 households almost overnight. By 1973, the parish had built a large multipurpose building in addition to the small frame country church that is still used, and boasted 1500 households. To facilitate the building of community, the parish was divided into 10 neighborhoods. Convinced that Christianity is an adult religion and that one priest had need of pastoral assistance, the pastor first hired two staff members—a director of adult education and a parish worker (a Sister who did everything pastoral that a priest would do except administer the sacraments).

Additions were made to the staff regularly as the parish grew and became more organized. When I arrived in the summer of 1973, the staff already consisted of a director of adult education, two teen ministers, a social action coordinator, a liturgist, two parish workers, and an associate pastor. I was hired to develop a family program and direct the existing preschool and elementary programs. Parishioners were basically young families with a median adult age between 30 and 40. Most were young executives and professional people in the middle to upper-middle class economic status with an educational background of at least some college. What impressed me most about the parish was the openness of staff and parishioners, and the community spirit that existed in the parish.

The official title of the parish is *The Parish Community of St. Joseph*. The strongest emphasis the first five years after the parish experienced its rapid growth was on community building, which was evidenced in the people's attitude toward one another and the parish in general.

This profile of the parish, coupled with my findings in visiting with families figured strongly in the design of our family program.

Once the design was determined, we began publicizing the program. Prior to registration for our education programs, I wrote three bulletin columns explaining the rationale behind family catechesis and the particular structure our program would assume. I also had open meetings with parents, introducing myself and the concept. I have vivid memories of those open meetings and can still hear myself saying:

"Theoretically, this concept makes a tremendous amount of sense. As I look back on my own religious development, I have to say that my family had the greatest amount of influence on my faith development as a child, and many of you have shared that same feeling here tonight. A good theory ought to be workable in the practical realm, but this one hasn't been tried in many places or for very long. Personally, I really believe that family catechesis is the direction we as a Church should go if we are concerned about the religious development of our children. I have no proof for you that it will work any better than our present system; but I think it will and ask you to risk with me and give it a try. I am sure that the result will not be worse, and I have a great deal of hope that it will be better. Will you risk with me?"

PFL's First Year

Thirty-five families did risk with me that first year. Twenty of them were families that I had met and talked with personally in my informal needs assessment, and with very few exceptions, those families have continued to participate in the program.

The times when a child asks a question are precisely moments for effective catechesis. They provide the parents an opportunity to explore more deeply their own adult faith, invite the parents to express that faith to their children, and reinforce the notion that faith grows through questioning and search.

At the end of the first year, one of the families learned that they were being transferred temporarily but would be back in a year and a half. Before leaving, the parents approached me after the Sunday Eucharistic liturgy, presented me with a $100 check and the admonition to use it for the continued development of PFL so they could rejoin the program when they returned. The second year, as in marriage and child rearing, is often the most difficult, and I have a suspicion that I might have given up the program if it hadn't been for that check and admonition—and about 50 supportive families, too; but that story later.

The structure of the program was simple, strongly resembling the peer-centered model and involving two meetings a month for participants. The first meeting was an adult workshop; the second was a children's workshop. There were three family celebrations offered in the course of the year. Using a general yearly theme, each of the workshops, which were offered from October to May, focused on a particular aspect of the theme.

Our theme that first year was *The Liturgical Year,* which is an ideal theme with which to begin a family program because it presents natural occasions for families to begin attempting some family home activities and experiences which can facilitate faith sharing, prayer and ritual. The liturgical theme also provides opportunities for the director of the program to affirm the activities that families have as part of their seasonal customs. Almost every family has some special traditions during the holidays which they seldom consider apropos to the faith and religious development of their members. As a result of the parents sharing these customs, receiving affirmation for their efforts, they slowly begin to realize that family catechesis is not so foreign to their families after all, but something they have been engaged in all along.

Another advantage of the liturgical theme is that it is relatively easy to design seasonal celebrations for both home and the parish center.

There are a number of ways that one might approach the theme of *The Liturgical Year.* Parents repeatedly expressed to me during the needs assessment a concern about prayer—the parents' own prayer life, as well as their teaching their children to pray and to share family prayer. All of them wanted to initiate some sort of family prayer, but they didn't know quite how to approach it or accomplish it. The experience the majority of parents had had with family prayer was the family rosary, which for most of them was an unpleasant memory and not one to which they wanted to subject their children.

Another concern expressed was the desire that both parents and children be able to understand the celebration of the Eucharist better.

With that information in mind, I approached the theme from the point of view of "Praying the Liturgical Year." The topic outline for the adult workshops was as follows:

1. *Appreciation of Creation*
   Private prayer. How shall I teach my child to pray?

2. *Thanksgiving/Liturgical Prayer in General*
   Public worship, the great prayer of praise and thanks. How can public worship become more meaningful in our family?
3. *Advent—Christmas*
   How can our family better prepare for Christmas?
4. *Understanding Scripture*
   How can the Word of God become a living prayer in my life and how can I transmit that love and reverence for the Word to my family?
5. *Lent*
   How can Lent be a more prayerfully meaningful season for our family?
6. *Understanding the Mass*
   How can the Eucharist become a more meaningful family celebration for our family?
7. *Pentecost*
   Why have people called the present time "The Age of the Spirit"? What does this mean for my family?

The children's workshops also followed this topical outline. The three family celebrations

charistic liturgy connected with the program each year.

The first year's theme was the impetus for another PFL tradition which turned into a total parish tradition. To aid families in the celebration of Advent and Lent at home, the parish staff put together an Advent and a Lenten family activity booklet with numerous suggestions for ways that families could make those seasons more meaningful in their homes. (See "Celebrating the Seasons," Chapter 8.) When PFL families saw them, they suggested that we send copies to everyone in the parish; and we did.

For the second and third years, we revised the booklets. However, instead of mailing them to all members of the parish, we simply put them at the church entrance for families to pick up if they so wished. It was our way of testing how many people would be interested enough to pick up a booklet with the thought of using it at home. Over 1000 copies were taken home. There were about 1600 families in the parish at that time and we had made 800 copies, thinking that would be sufficient. Fortunately for all concerned, we began distribution two weeks prior to Advent, so we had time to print more, and families had time to

---

From the very beginning PFL was adult centered, because we firmly believe that a family is only as healthy as the adults in the family.

---

took place during Advent, Lent, and in May. The May family celebrations were the beginning of a PFL tradition that we have repeated every year since: our PFL Family Picnic/Pot Luck. The first year the picnic was preceded by a session about Pentecost being the birthday of the Church and then we celebrated a Eucharistic liturgy. Since then, we have had just a picnic and a final (usually the only) Eu-

plan their activities before the first Sunday of the season.

The fourth year we did little revision, used a stiffer cover, and asked families to keep the booklets for future years. They now pack them away in safe places each year and bring them out again the following year. It becomes a family tragedy when one is lost. We reprint a few copies each year for new parishioners and for those families who put their copies away in *too safe* a place!

An alternate idea which can produce basically the same result is to collect the various traditions of families and compile them into a parish Advent/Lenten booklet, including the names and phone numbers of the families who submitted the idea. The staff can also add their suggestions. Then, if there is need for further explanation, families can call one another.

Such an exchange is good for community building, affirms families as well as generates new ideas for those families who would like to do something special for the season but don't know where or how to begin. The project could be the follow-up of a parent meeting in advance of the season and would be an easy way to accomplish the same result we had in a smaller parish or a parish with only one coordinator or perhaps no coordinator.

The adult workshops have always been considered the most important component of the program. From the very beginning, the aim of PFL was adult centered, because we firmly believe that a family is only as healthy as the adults in that family. Parents are, as Bettye Lechner says, "the architects of the family

include a theological examination of the topic for the month, practical applications for living that theology as adults and as parents of a family, and the communication and parenting skills related to the sharing of that lived experience at home.

For example, the workshop on the topic of private prayer mentioned above included a look at prayer from a theological and traditional point of view, an examination of private prayer today with specific emphasis on its many forms, a discussion of possibilities for prayer alone, couple prayer, and finally some particular suggestions on how to encourage children to pray.

I gave one specific suggestion as "homework," in connection with the last mentioned session (and I prefer to make the home activities optional). I suggested that each parent begin the custom of tracing a sign of the cross on their children's foreheads each night when they tuck them into bed, and say something like: "God bless you," "I love you," "I thank God for you." This simple action affects both the child and the parents in positive ways. It helps develop a sense of prayerfulness and peace at bedtime. In a sense, it erases any unpleasantness that may have occurred be-

Basically, Project Family Life is a program designed to challenge the priorities of parents and families, aid the faith growth of parents, and affirm them and their efforts toward sharing that faith.

and the major faith influence in the lives of their children." A community of believers is created only when the adults in that community realize that being Christian requires freely accepting and choosing to witness Christ.

The adult workshops are the one constant of PFL since its inception. It is the one phase of the program that parents specifically have asked to remain unchanged. The workshops

tween parent and child that day. It enables parents to pay particular attention to each child, which children love. It says something to the child about the parents' sense of God and prayer, and it very quickly becomes a family tradition that children will not allow parents to forget.

The following month at least five parents came to the adult workshop reporting that their children asked for their parents' blessing as the parents were leaving the house because they would be asleep when their parents returned that night. In time, children will begin to ask their parents to explain why they perform the action, what was the meaning of the words that they used. Some children will even insist on returning the blessing to the parents. The action can also be the impetus for additional bedtime prayer. Suddenly parents notice that they are teaching their children prayer more naturally and comfortably than they had ever anticipated.

covered in the workshops. Parents came about 15 minutes early to pick up their children and join in the prayer-ritual. (Well, if I am to be honest, I would have to say that parents came to watch, because the ritual was definitely child centered and we all have a tendency as adults to simply observe when something is purely child centered.)

The children's workshops were not my idea of good family catechesis; but in my visits with parents, they indicated that they wanted something specifically structured for their children. The family celebrations that were

---

To really proclaim is to speak, act, dance, skip, stoop to help, reach to accept, and be silent to watch and pray.

Parents need most these very simple, yet practical kinds of communication and parenting skills. We might be tempted to inundate them with psychological principles of parenting, but they will more readily attempt and will experience the most success with the pragmatic, down-to-earth suggestions. I am aware of 12- and 13-year-olds today, whose parents began this custom six years ago, who will not go to bed without their parents' blessing.

The children's workshops also followed the topic outline for the year, with workshops offered for grades one to 12. Each couple in the program was expected to teach one of the children's sessions once during the year, and I taught the eight seventh to twelfth graders who were in the program. That meant, of course, that I had to prepare lesson plans for each grade level and conduct teacher-training sessions with a new group of parent-teachers each month.

At the conclusion of each of the children's sessions, we would all gather for a final prayer or ritual related to the topic that had been

offered as options (which, interestingly, most families attended), were given much thought and serious planning in conjunction with our liturgist. I wanted them to be exceptionally good experiences for families. In my mind they were serving as an example of what might be possible instead of children's workshops. No one knew that, however, except myself.

Working with the small group of junior and senior high students was particularly enlightening and led me to believe that a separate session for that age group was valuable. I used basically the same outline that I used with the adults, but with an approach and activities geared to their age level. I was amazed at their interest and hunger for the theological content I gave them. They had been subjected to the collage-making era of elementary religious education, and while they had heard about some of the concepts we investigated, they didn't really understand them. That was to my benefit, since it led to a rich openness and desire to begin to understand and learn. Unfortunately, they didn't have very valuable experiences of the concepts, so at times it was difficult to base the knowledge on experiences.

I have never been asked so many intelligent questions by a group of young people their age. There was seldom any absenteeism, and in the years that followed, most of them chose to attend the more content-oriented offerings that were a part of PFL and our parish youth programs rather than the other offerings we had for adolescents, which were more experiential, communication-oriented programs. Four of the original eight who were in the group enrolled in Catholic colleges in order to be able to continue some theological study along with regular collegiate courses. I found this particularly gratifying, since very few of our young people choose to continue their education at Catholic institutions, (apart from financial reasons) because their parish grade or high schools do not provide them with impetus to continue in Catholic colleges. Each of these four considers their Catholic college education important enough for them to work on campus and at double summer jobs to help their parents with expenses. Appropriate to their development, the theology that they received during their time in PFL and what they are receiving in college is coming at a time in their lives when the information can help them make some critical faith decisions.

For that reason I often tell parents that in my opinion and from my experience, a Catholic school education is most valuable at the college level. Prior to that time, children need to see and experience the faith life of a Christian family and Christian community so that they have some values and attitudes to test against the theological information.

Parents whose youngsters are at Catholic colleges today beam when they see me and share tales about their children's theological pursuits, usually adding, ''We're going to be in hock for awhile, Sister, but I think you were right; they're getting their theology now and loving it.''

What I enjoy most about our budding theologians is their desire to get together with me during their breaks to discuss the theology they're studying and to share campus quips.

PFL's Second Year

PFL's first year was a glorious success. All 35 families agreed to return the following year, and most of them conducted the summer recruitment program which I described earlier. Ninety families participated in the second-year program. While we were somehow spared horrendous errors the first year, we were not so fortunate the second. We were obviously very pleased with ourselves over our magnificent success; so, when a priest on sabbatical asked to spend a year learning about family catechesis in our parish, we were honored. Since I believe that a person learns best by doing, I invited him to be an integral part of the program. We decided that he and I could teach the adult workshops, which were offered on two nights of the week to facilitate smaller groups and provide an option for the parents. He could help plan and execute the family celebrations and visit the children's classes.

Teamwork demands time spent in communicating ideas, brainstorming, sharing visions and dreams, and planning together. The priest and I did not do a sufficient amount of that. In fact, looking back, I suspect that I really didn't even do a very good job of explaining the basic philosophy and the hoped-for future of the program to him. We tended to spend only a small amount of time discussing the approach to the topics we would cover, planned alone our separate sections, leaving copies of our notes on each other's desks, and being surprised at one another's presentations when it came time for the workshops. As it turned out, we were coming from different philosophical and educational backgrounds in terms of family catechesis in particular and religious education in general.

Very early in the year, I became exceedingly angry at both of us, but didn't do anything constructive about it. The conflict between us became obvious to the adults in the program, and I must say, I was surprised that we still had 50 families participating in the program by the end of the year. I am not very gracious at failing, and if it had not been for the support that I received from my pastor, the staff, and those 50 families, I probably would not be able to tell this story now. In evaluating the year with participants, I explained, as best I could, what seemed to have happened. Their response was heartwarming and unanimous; "We'll stick with it if you will."

Those who were in the program for the second year reminded me of our first year. Those who had joined the second year agreed to stay with it in the hope of having an experience like that which had been described to them by their peer community members. Choking back tears through their hugs and words of encouragement and support, I took a deep breath, and a summer off for study. The participants did the rest. They conducted an informal recruitment to the program all summer and in early fall used the pulpit for about five minutes to explain what PFL meant to them as families. I returned from my summer off to be met by 75 families ready to participate in the program for the third year.

Not everything about the second year was unfortunate. By December of that year, my secret ambition regarding the children's workshops was realized, much sooner than I had imagined. After the December children's workshop, a group of about 20 teaching-parents literally backed me into a corner and said, "These children's workshops are useless." About half of them had just experienced the pre-Christmas discipline problems that those of us who have taught know all about. They proceeded to cite existing situations which made the workshops less than successful: They were held in the evening when children were physically tired and tired of school. The children were often missing favorite TV programs and opportunities to spend time together with their families, consequently, causing a problem in terms of discipline and concentration. The children had different teachers each time, which seemed to the parents to cause continuity problems for both children and teachers. Some of the parents

who taught were dismal failures as teachers.

I also think that our theme and topics for the year were a part of the problem, too. Our theme for the second year had been *Covenant-Commitment*. Our topic outline, while interesting to adults, was a bit much for the elementary-aged child.

We had committed many of the errors I

Teamwork demands time spent in communicating ideas, brainstorming, sharing visions and dreams, and planning together.

---

warned against in Chapters 1 and 2.

Finally, the children themselves had strongly indicated that they much preferred the family celebrations when the whole family came together and the last 15 minutes of each children's workshop, when their parents were there with them, rather than the workshops they came to alone.

The solution, according to this delegation of parents, was to drop the children's workshops as of January and have an adult workshop and a family workshop which was similar to the family celebrations and the prayer-rituals at the conclusion of each of the children's workshops.

I was ecstatic but hid my ecstasy by asking some critical questions such as: "Is it all right with you if your children don't get that formal religious education? Do you know how difficult it is to plan a workshop that involves all age groups? Will you all help implement and participate in the family workshops?"

The answers to all of my questions were in the affirmative. I believed in their earnestness over this situation. However, still playing my "devil's advocate" role, I continued to protest the difficulty of planning family workshops until the parents informed me that I would have more time since I didn't have to develop lesson plans and conduct teacher training sessions. And, they reminded me, "We're paying you to give us what we need." I had used those very words in the first months of PFL to help them realize that it was their program and not mine. I must have done a convincing job! The words were coming back to me.

I relate this little charade purposely. One of the things that I have learned working with families for eight years is that it is advantageous to all concerned if as director you are not totally knowledgeable and capable of all things, that the parents realize they contribute positively to the direction, implementation, and ultimately to the continued success of the program. That evening I went home pleased that families themselves came to the point of recommending the kind of program model that I would have liked from the very beginning.

But perhaps such a model might not have worked from the very beginning. Respecting the process and timing in others is so important in any decision that calls for commitment from them. At this point, which was my teachable moment with the parents, family catechesis was being actualized. The participants were assuming responsibility for their own program. It wasn't my program even if I was the PFL Lady; it was theirs. Since that time, I capitalized on every opportunity that I could to remind them that they saw the need for a structure change and it made for better programs.

So often I hear the phrase, "What do I know? I'm just a parent." The statement may seem trite, even humorous, but I think it expresses a real inadequacy parents feel. Helping parents to realize that they do know a great deal about what is best for them and their children is extremely important. One of the phrases that I have used, which helps parents come to that realization in a humorous but pointed way is: "What do I know? I'm just a nun." They recognize their own statement in mine.

I also made a point of telling parents from the very beginning of the program that there was nothing wrong with telling their children, "I don't know." I reminded them that I was only a phone call away, and they could call any time. Together we would try to come up with adequate explanations to their children's questions. And questions I have received, questions precipitated by family workshops, family activities, rituals, the Sunday Liturgy, family prayer, and by seemingly nothing in particular but a child's imagination: "What's God's middle name?" "How old is God?" "Does God cry?" "If God is invisible, how can Jesus see him?" "How come God invented Mass?" "When can I have one of those flat potato chips?" "How does God get food?" "Why does God make things that hurt people?" "Why did those men kill Jesus?" "Where is heaven?" "Did the men who killed Jesus go to heaven?" "If I'm part of this community, why can't I have blessed bread, too?" "What's so good about Good Friday?"

Such questions, as difficult as they seem to answer, are precisely moments for effective catechesis. They provide the parents an opportunity to explore more deeply their own

The nuclear family is now a minority in our culture, and our programs must reflect these shifts and changes in societal reality.

adult faith, invite the parents to express that faith to their children, and reinforce the notion that faith grows through questioning and search.

Because family catechesis is such a new experience, parents find themselves "growing

---

Parents who begin family catechetical programs when their children are older have a decidedly more difficult time with family faith-sharing home activities and ritualizing than do families who begin with young children.

---

up'' with their children. Parents who begin family catechetical programs when their children are older have a decidedly more difficult time with family faith-sharing home activities and ritualizing than do families who begin with young children.

Both parents and older children feel uncomfortable and often embarrassed trying these new family experiences. With young children, parents can try almost anything, and the only ones experiencing embarrassment are the parents, who can discuss and come to grips with the feelings, and even grow in faith together through their sharing them with each other.

Directors of family programs can aid parents in overcoming that self-consciousness, often simply by listening empathetically and sharing their own similar feelings. I have often related to parents my own feelings of discomfort when my family gets together and I am asked to lead prayer or some family ritual that was ours when we were children and is now re-activated for the grandchildren who are all under 11.

One night at an adult workshop a couple told an interesting story that I think speaks to this situation. They had been in PFL a year and never attempted any family activities or rituals. Each of the parents had wanted to suggest something, but each was sure the other parent would be embarrassed and uncomfortable. Finally, one night while the mother was at work, the father decided to initiate a family experience that had been suggested as part of the program. The attempt was successful, he thought, based on the responses of the six children.

A few nights later, when Dad was gone for the evening, Mom decided to try to initiate the same activity, found the children enthusiastically agreeing, offering further suggestions, and sharing what had happened earlier during the same activity with their father. The parents discussed their mutual assumption later that evening, and the decision was made to continue family activities with both parents present. Embarrassment and reluctance are more often the problem for adults rather than children.

For that reason, as well as many others, I believe very strongly that an adult approach and an early start in family catechesis are essential. The Bishop's Statement on Early Childhood Care and Education, *Let the Little Children Come to Me* says it well: ''Assisting families with young children today would reduce the need for remedial and rehabilitative programs tomorrow. . . . The Church must reaffirm its own commitment to early childhood care . . . and to education for parenthood.''

Families with older children, particularly children in their early teens, can sometimes convince their older children to help plan and conduct the family activities, but even this approach is not always successful. The families with older children continued to have problems in the program. I wish now that I had encouraged only families with young children to participate in the program. Furthermore, family rituals and activities are most valuable when they are introduced to children when they are young because, then as they become older and more autonomous, they have some valuable experience on which to base the values, attitudes and lifestyles with which they are experimenting.

During the second year, we continued to offer the teen workshops with a married couple from the program leading the sessions. The teens, however, balked at coming to the family workshops, maintaining that the workshops were too elementary for them. Neither parents nor I believed that to be true, but I suspect that the presence of so many younger children and so few young people their own age was really the deterring factor. Consequently we decided that the family workshop could be optional for teens, and parents suggested that senior high people could be invited to the adult workshops. A few teenagers chose one or other of these alternatives. In general, however, the majority of teenagers did not choose to join in either of them but did attend the teen workshop which was divided later into a junior high and a senior high group because of the numbers attending the workshop. The junior high sessions were taught by a married couple in the program and the senior high sessions were conducted by the senior high youth minister.

PFL's Third Year

The third year of the program was the best year. It was definitely the most pleasant year for me, and the year that offered the most to the participants in terms of approach and stability of structure. A time comes in family catechesis when the program structure becomes just right for awhile, and the third, fourth, and fifth years seemed to be that time for PFL.

In the spring of our disconcerting second year, Mike, our parish liturgist, approached me with the request to work with me in the program. He saw the development of family faith life in the community as integral to the development and effectiveness of parish liturgical life and felt that his involvement in family catechesis would be an asset to his coordination of the community's liturgical celebrations. I had worked with Mike for two years. We had become good friends. We shared sim-

ilar philosophies of ministry, education, and life. Our theologies were alike or at least complementary. We were both avid students of liturgy, and we both reveled in the study and enjoyment of the literary and artistic. In addition, Mike had, among other talents, that of being a gifted musician. He also was more theologically knowledgeable than I regarding the theme we had chosen for the coming year: *Morality and Moral Development.*

I agreed to give it a try. We prepared and team taught the adult workshops and planned and executed the family workshops together. Our topic outline was as follows:

1. *Introduction to Christian Life and Christian Morality*
   Christian life as gift, and invitation; personal response as membership in Church and as Christian morality.
2. *Prayer*
   Prayer as a response to life. Active-contemplative prayer, children's prayer, family prayer.
3. *Moral Development in Children*
   Conscience formation, birth to adolescence from a psychological and religious point of view.
4. *Moral Development of Adults*
   Working with the formed conscience—adolescent to adult.
5. *Grace and the Human Condition*
   Grace builds on nature—or does it?
6. *Specific moral and ethical topics chosen by participants*

The team approach this time was excellent. We took the time to plan together, and we worked well together. Participants appreciated and grew from the dual approach to topics. We obviously enjoyed working together, and in a sense, we were modeling for them what could happen in their homes. The male-female complementariness was a definite asset to the program. Each of us felt a certain security knowing that the other was there to expound, provide additional explanation, comment upon, and even express an alternate idea about the topics being discussed in the workshops. We each met differing needs in the participants because of our specific teaching techniques.

I was surprised to learn that Mike's approach was not always the one most appreciated by the men, nor was mine always the technique most beneficial to the women; in fact, it was often the opposite. The unanimous opinion at the end of the year was that the team approach definitely enhanced the program and was valued by the families. If you have the personnel, I strongly encourage a male-female team approach to augment your family program. But, obviously, a male and female will not necessarily be a team. Personality and commitment are two important factors.

Another advantage of our team approach was that as the year progressed, the family workshops became less *learning* experiences and more and more *ritual* experiences. As a result of this change of focus, we found parents becoming more personally involved in the family workshops as opposed to being parentally involved, or involved with a sense of trying to provide a learning situation for their children. Learning was indeed still taking place, but in a much *different* way, and in a manner that provided faith sharing opportunities for the whole family and not just occasions for parents to share their faith with their children.

Children, too, became family members who had faith to share. Mike and I also began sharing more than just our intellectual or creative and organizational selves. We, too, shared our faith. We all saw one another in a slightly different light and were becoming a community within a community.

At the end of the year we had buttons made up that said, "We are a PFL family." This was both response to a spirit that was developing among us and a publicity technique along with the printing of a brochure expressing the aim, rationale, and structure of the program, as well as reactions from people in the program. Other parishioners naturally asked about the buttons, heard about the program from children, adults and the brochure, and

began asking specific questions about the program. The enrollment grew from 100 families the third year to 130 families the next year.

PFL's Fourth Year

The fourth year was again a solo year for me. Mike had entered the seminary; Dean (the teen minister) had gone to graduate school; Jim took a job as liturgist in another parish; and I experienced the grieving process three or four times over that year because I never really allowed myself the luxury of going through it once completely. It was a year of emotional contrasts for me, but a good year for the program.

My job responsibilities were changed. Instead of coordinating the preschool and elementary programs along with PFL, I assumed the coordination of the adult education program, and someone else was hired to coordinate the children's programs. I was pleased with the change. I was finding it decidedly more difficult to believe in the philosophy of a preschool and elementary religious education program, and I have always believed in the value of adult growth and enrichment. But the absence of the team members who had been so helpful to me left an enormous void in my life.

PFL workshops were being repeated on four different nights of the week by this time, in order to facilitate smaller groups and provide families with optional nights from which to choose. While I found the schedule personally taxing, it was a necessity considering the number of families involved.

Each of the previous years I had prepared a bibliography for adults with most of the books listed being available in the parish library. This year I also used a general text that was given to each family, Monika Hellwig's *The Meaning of the Sacraments* (Pflaum Press). The teen portion of the program was dropped this fourth year because all of our parish education programs were following the same theme, and we recommended that PFL teens be involved in the regular teen programs of the parish.

Having the total parish concentrate on the same theme each year facilitates a family approach to all of catechesis in the parish. In this way, all members of the family involved in some form of parish catechesis are following basically the same outline. Knowing that, parents can initiate family discussions about that particular topic, and suggestions for home activities can be sent to families through the various programs or through the parish bulletin each month. Similarly, the parish library can feature particular books, articles, tapes, etc. as resource materials for the month. Liturgy and social action are other aspects of parish life that can utilize the same theme.

The concept of wholistic parish catechesis was a suggestion that I made the year I came to St. Joseph's, but one which did not take shape in a workable way until four years later. Then it lasted only one year. The idea takes much time, total team ownership, and a lot of parish planning and organization to accomplish.

We have not given up completely on the idea. Some of the parish programs do follow a common theme, but not all do. At St. Joseph's we have seven religious education programs from which people can choose (adult, family, senior high, junior high, elementary, preschool, and special education). The integration of all of these programs plus the other areas of ministry in the parish has been a constant problem for us with no easy solutions. Presently, we are in the process of doing some restructuring of our educational staff and programs in an attempt to facilitate that integration. As a beginning, we are trying to integrate activities during the major liturgical seasons of Advent and Lent. Perhaps occasional integration is the most we can ever achieve.

At the beginning of our fourth year, Dolores Curran visited our parish. Her talk on the importance of family catechesis and family ritual provided the impetus for the rest of our year. Having her speak added the benefit of someone else reiterating the thoughts and ideas that we had been sharing with the parish

Parents need most these very simple yet practical kinds of communication and parenting skills.

I suggested that each parent begin the custom of tracing the sign of the cross on their children's foreheads each night when they tuck them into bed, and saying something like, "I love you" or "I thank God for you."

for three years. The topics the rest of the year included:

1. *Sacraments in general*
   Shifts in understanding sacraments since Vatican II
2. *Sacraments of Initiation*
   A study of Baptism, Confirmation, Eucharist
3. *Eucharist*
   A more detailed look at the sacrament which is the summit of our Christian life
4. *The Sacrament of Reconciliation*
   An investigation into the idea of sin, reconciliation, penance and the new rite of the sacrament

5. *Sacraments of Vocation*
   A study of Matrimony and Holy Orders
6. *Sacraments of Anointing*
   A study of the Sacrament of the Anointing of the Sick and a further look into the other sacraments that involve anointing

The study of sacraments is one of my favorite topics, and that proved to be a definite advantage in the program that year. Not only

non with some of them, they pointed out something about the program of which I was not cognizant.

One married couple put it succinctly: "You gave us a lot in a year or two, Sister. We needed a year off to assimilate and try some of the things we didn't have a chance to try, and we wanted to practice some of the things you kept encouraging us to do. So we decided not to be involved in the program this year and instead want to just try living what we've

---

Helping people remember and revive their ethnic customs can be a great service to families as well as being actual catechesis on liturgy; for remembering is what we are about as we gather for the breaking of the bread.

---

were the adult workshops especially enjoyable to both myself and the participants, but the family rituals too were particularly meaningful to all of us. We celebrated a ritual of community, a ritual of Baptism by immersion of one of the newest members of the program, a ritual of family reconciliation, a Parents' Day ritual that was totally planned and executed by the children in the program, and a sacramental Anointing of the Sick to which families brought sick grandparents, neighbors, friends and relatives, and participated fully in the laying on of hands and anointing of those people.

By the fourth year I was noticing a trend in PFL that at first caused me some anxiety. While most of the initial 35 families stayed with the program continuously over the four years, other families joined, dropped out and, in several cases, returned after a year or two. My initial reaction was to try to determine what I might have done wrong to cause them to leave. But when I discussed the phenome-

learned, and being involved in other parish and civic activities."

I was gratified to learn that the program had become that kind of catalyst for further family involvement and that it served as a living experience for families.

Over the years, families were encouraged through home activities and workshop follow-up suggestions to extend their faith sharing to others through our Social Action program and through greater involvement in Liturgy and pastoral care. We are fortunate to have viable programs and excellent coordinators who readily incorporate families into the mainstreams of their ministry.

PFL families took on such activities as organizing our parish Social Action Center's food shelf, which provides emergency food for the needy in the area, visiting nursing homes, shopping for and delivering holiday meals for families who otherwise would have a skimpy holiday fare, choosing and wrapping Christmas gifts that were subsequently distributed by the Social Action Center, working as families in the parish Social Action free clothing store, etc.

Before long we realized that PFL families were becoming the most active members of the community. Many PFL parents were teaching in our more structured religious education programs, even though their children were not a part of those programs. Ushering, or "hosting" as we call it, was becoming a family function for PFL families rather than just Dad's involvement. The children of PFL families were obviously the children most comfortable and enthusiastic at parish activities, children's experiences in the parish, and special family and children's liturgies which we offered periodically.

One mother, whose family were members of PFL for three years, taught a fifth grade elementary religious education class one year and chose to have her own son in her class. She found that in spite of a seeming lack of instruction in doctrine, her son was the most knowledgeable in the class, at least in terms of sacraments, which is what fifth graders studied in that particular curriculum. That was prior to the year that we investigated sacraments in the family program.

By the fourth year, parents were sharing many of the activities and rituals that they were initiating as families and in many cases were involving other families with them for neighborhood family activities. Two married couples took a scripture course offered through our adult enrichment program one year. Their children, observing their parents studying and discussing the scriptures, asked to be included in the discussion and study; and before long, the family had set aside one night a week for family bible study. Their discussions were obviously less adult than the parents' discussions, since their children were under 12 years old, but both families found the experiences most gratifying.

In one neighborhood, a group of families together planned three family activities during Christmas vacation one year; these have become traditions for them now. Their activities include a sleigh ride, a skating party, and a game night around the fireplace in one family's home. Other families go camping or cross-country skiing together. Some families in one neighborhood gather on a regular basis for an evening of prayer and faith sharing. One father whose job often involves travel during the week arranges to spend every Saturday morning with one of his four children. They begin the day by having breakfast out and then doing whatever the child wants to do for the rest of the morning. Every month, each of his children has an entire morning alone with his/her father. His sharing of that activity was a strong impetus for several other fathers and mothers to spend quality time with their children individually.

Many of these activities seem unrelated to religious experience. It takes a long time for parents to value such activities as *teachable moments* and moments of genuine faith sharing. Over the years, I made a point of providing time during the adult workshops for the sharing of family experiences of the type mentioned, so that I could once again reaffirm the value of parents and children simply being together and enjoying one another and that time being a God-filled moment. Taking the time to do that also gave the other parents ideas for activities their families might also attempt, and it gave me the opportunity to stress repeatedly the integration of religion and spirituality into the everyday lived situation.

Our religion and culture have unfortunately done a very good job of separating body and soul, religion and secular actions, so my emphasis on simple, very natural home experiences and the teachable moment became a constant reiteration in the program in an attempt to correct the strong conditioning to separate the two. Also, I tried to disestablish the idea that family catechesis meant moving the classroom into the home, which is often the predisposition with which parents come into a family program.

The successes of the third and fourth year, the involvement of PFL families in the total life of the parish, and my ardor over the kinds of family and neighborhood experiences that were taking place regrettably had an unfortunate side effect. Because of the enthusiasm of PFL families, they were most often chosen to be the more active participants in liturgies and parish activities. They were also the parishioners usually called upon to aid in the development of various projects. They were most often there, usually ready with an affirmative response, and the program structure offered a regular forum through which the other areas of ministry could reach people easily. Among the staff, PFL and I were coming to be known as "Sister Sandy and her *creme de la creme.*"

The fact was, and still is, that PFL does attract the more active members of the community. It is a program that presupposes a relatively healthy and secure family and people who are willing to risk an untraditional religious education model and theory. They are the natural leaders in the community.

The type of parishioner that the program attracts and our own fervor over their growth and involvement began to cause some parish discontent, and we quickly recognized that if we didn't cool our jets a bit, we could have a parish division similar to the Catholic school-CCD dichotomy. The situation also made us more aware of the need, in a parish our size, for more than one model of family catechesis, and also the need for something to meet the needs of families who were not yet ready for any kind of family catechesis.

We hired a coordinator of family growth and enrichment to respond to those needs the year PFL was five years old. This person coordinates family and couple communication opportunities, family growth groups, family clusters, family counseling, family enrichment days and other forms of family ministry to offer other options for families not attracted to PFL. Her work with families has already led families, who didn't think they could cope with the expectations of PFL, into the program after some counseling or participation in her programming.

We no longer pass out PFL buttons, refer less to PFL accomplishments, guard our enthusiasm about our being *creme de la creme,* and are more conscious to praise all parish programs. The fact that PFL families are the more actively involved parishioners cannot be denied, but we are learning to do what parents have to do all the time, and that is to be equally sensitive to all of their children, and more encouraging to the less assertive or adventuresome.

Some of our zeal over the growth and involvement of PFL families was expressed for publicity purposes, and that may not have been the best technique for public relations.

I relate this realization that we came to as a precautionary measure for others planning or involved in some form of family catechesis. It is an easy error to make, and one that can be detrimental to both family catechesis and to the parish.

PFL's Fifth Year

I moved into the fifth year of PFL with a conscious awareness of the situation, 150 participating families, a theme of ministry, and a subcommittee of families who helped me plan and implement the family workshops. The structure of the program was again altered slightly that year. Parents were becoming more secure with their use and evaluation of family time at home, and suggested that Advent and Lent be free of workshops so that they could implement some of the suggestions in the Advent and Lenten Family Activity Booklets to a greater degree in their homes. We also incorporated an optional Family Weekend Experience in April for 20 families on a first come-first served basis.

The Weekend Experience was held at the parish center using the format of the *Family Weekend Experience Kit* designed by Marriage Encounter and published by Sadlier. Both of the modifications in the program structure were advantageous and appreciated by the participants. The following year, the Family Weekend Experience was held for a larger number of families, at a retreat center, which allowed a weekend totally away from home for the participating families.

The attitude of shared responsibility for the program and the open, enthusiastic spirit of the families seemed to me to be particularly evident the fifth year. Perhaps it was because we had been working together for five years, a novel occurrence for both of us. Coordinators in the past had not stayed in the parish longer than three years, nor had I been in one parish more than three years. Perhaps it was because I was aware that it would be the last year that I would be involved in the direction of PFL. Perhaps it was the topics covered. Perhaps it was because I had gone on record as having announced to all of the couples in the program that I was no longer unsure of the workableness of a family approach to catechesis, because we had together shown that it was a viable theory that did work, if accompanied by more than a modicum of effort, time, risk, and energy.

Whatever the reasons, the fifth year seemed to be our most joyously tranquil year. We all seemed to have reached a comfort level with one another that allowed for a greater repartee at workshops and an even more vibrant response of families toward the continued growth of the program.

Our outline included:

1. *The Gathering of the Gifted*
   A look at the gifts of the Spirit and our own particular gifts given us for the good of others.
2. *"Everyone a Minister"*
   An investigation of the priesthood of all believers and its meaning for us all as ministers in the Church and world community.
3. *Family Ministry*
   Possibilities for the average American family today both within and outside the structure of the Church.
4. *Confirmation and Ministry*

Our text for the year was *Everyone a Minister* by Otto Feucht (Concordia Publishers), a marvelous little book on the priesthood of believers. Our family workshops included a determination of individual and family gifts, an anointing for ministry, the keeping and sharing of family ministry logs, drama, dance, a sense of joy, and a marked lack of concern

about whether or not children were getting enough doctrine. It was almost as if parents were beginning to experience the results of five years of faith growth in themselves and their children, and were enjoying the dividends with an ease and calmness I had not noticed before.

At the April evaluation nights, I announced to each group that I would not be directing

---

Before long we realized that PFL families were becoming the most active members in the parish community.

PFL anymore. After the delightfulness of the year, I found the announcement difficult to make but it would have been even more difficult had I been also leaving the parish and had Kathie, my replacement in the program, not been as competent as she is. Kathie was hired as full-time director of family catechesis, while I was to continue to direct the adult education on a part-time basis in the parish and do writing, lecturing and consulting in family catechesis in other parishes and dioceses.

After five years, PFL families were willing and able to share responsibility for the continued development of the program. I knew that they would see that the program continued in a manner that would serve them best.

I was witnessing a self-assuredness in parents that was more conspicuous than in previous years. One night, for example, at an adult workshop, I was responding to a question and eloquently expounding about a parenting technique based on good psychological principles. Unexpectedly a voice from the group interrupted with, "Wrong!" I was pleasantly amazed and resorted with my "What-do-I-know, I'm-just-a-nun" comment.

When the laughter subsided, the group

launched into a marvelous discussion which responded to the original question in a much more pragmatic manner than I could ever have given with my textbook psychology.

That kind of sharing and ministry with one another was becoming more and more common in the program. In addition, I felt it was time for new leadership. The program was ready for a new personality to avoid the possibility of becoming locked into a particular approach or becoming stagnant. We all need a change now and then in order to grow. I knew that I was ready for a change and I suspect that the families in the program were, too.

Disadvantages

PFL has many advantages, and, as with any model, some disadvantages. It does not, for example, attract singles and grandparents as does the family cluster model. It is not a model which will attract or involve all families of the parish. Designed to be most beneficial for young families, it does not always meet the needs of families with older children. It does serve the needs of some single parents, but not all of them; very much depends on the security and self-confidence of the parents. It has caused some parish devisiveness, but that was basically a staff fault that can be avoided.

Basically, PFL is a program designed to challenge the priorities of parents and families, aid the faith growth of parents and affirm them and their efforts toward sharing that faith. It has worked very well for the Parish Community of St. Joseph in New Hope, Minnesota. There may be aspects of it that are useful to you. Our successes may reassure you; our failures may offer you precautions, and our developmental process and thematic approach may help you in your own planning.

Project Family Life, as it exists at St. Joseph's, can never be exactly duplicated in any other parish, even if I were to go to another parish as its director, precisely because it is a program designed specifically for that parish and to a great extent designed by the participants in the program. It took a lot of work, time, and effort, a few tears, a great deal of

enthusiasm, plenty of research and study, support from parish team members and my own personal friends, belief in families and family catechesis, even when it seemed there was little in which to believe, an ability to listen as well as communicate ideas, a desire to support and affirm parents, and a sense of humor.

Other Possibilities

Your parish may need to start and proceed more slowly or more rapidly. You may or may not have a large staff with which to work. You will probably approach the whole concept in an entirely different way.

In a rural area, for example, I have always dreamed of reinstating the Rogation Days and developing a program around the natural cycle of the farming community. The blessing of the fields in the spring could begin with a special ritual at the church with copies of the ritual and containers of the water blessed for the ritual made available to each family so they can then go home and bless their own fields. The year could include a harvest ritual of thanks and praise with a blessing of animals, a new life workshop and ritual in the spring when the baby animals begin making their appearance.

These simple celebrations experienced the first year of the program can open the door for other family and parish activities in following years. Small rural parishes have the advantage of being able to incorporate family activities into the total life of the parish because of their size and the rooted community attitude of the people.

A small parish also can easily have a parish Passover or Seder Meal that can be preceded by some education about Passover and followed by education about Eucharist and liturgy, during the Lenten and Easter seasons. The first three years of PFL we had PFL Passovers. They were simple adaptations of the rite which moved into a celebration of the Liturgy of Eucharist at the Berakah or fourth cup of wine (See Chapter 9 on Family Rituals). When the group got too big to continue with the group Passover, we revised the ritual and made it available to families to celebrate at home. The experience with the group enabled families to feel more secure about trying the ritual in their homes.

Ethnic parishes have a wealth of possibilities for beginning a family approach, as well as contributions that they can make to those of us who live in "melting pot" parishes. The family and family catechesis was of paramount importance to our foremothers and forefathers. Most of us, if we research our ethnic heritage, can find numerous family traditions that served as catechesis for people.

Helping people remember and revive those customs can be a great service to families as well as being actual catechesis on liturgy, for remembering is what we are about as we gather for the breaking of the bread. Many of those ethnic customs are poignantly social action oriented and can serve as catechesis in that area also.

In one parish that is made up of four distinct ethnic groups, the people spent one whole year with each group researching and sharing the customs, traditions, rituals, music, costumes, foods, etc. of each nationality. Such sharing proved not only educational, but bonded the groups into a community, by easing some tensions and building understanding between the groups.

A friend of mine, who is a sister and professor of philosophy, comes from a small ethnic rural parish and has been spending several years returning to that parish during Advent, Lent and summer to work with the pastor and people in reviving the customs that she experienced as a child but which seem to have diminished drastically since then. Though not of her ethnic persuasion, I have accompanied her, helped and participated in some of the activities.

The young people of the parish are amazed at the richness of their background and the older people are thrilled with the affirmation that is given to traditions which for a time were considered unimportant by the Church. Gathering the elders of the parish for remembering and working with younger adults in re-

activating some traditions can accomplish the same kind of response as PFL and can be a good way to begin implementing a family approach to catechesis.

Parishes with schools seem to be the most reluctant to attempt family catechesis. The school easily can determine the parish priorities to the detriment of a more total parish catechesis. The problem exists whether families who have children in the school have also to participate in a family program. Some parents who "send their children to the Catholic school" consider their obligation to nurture faith thereby fulfilled. There is also the reluctance to hire a director of family catechesis because of lack of moneys available for the religious education of those families not in the school.

In parishes where there is a religious education director as well as a school staff, the problem becomes one of teamwork between DRE and school staff. A parish with a school must first solve those problems before any attempt toward family catechesis is made. Then, a family program must very definitely be open to the total parish and absolutely no distinction made between school families and other families. A great amount of adult education regarding the idea usually has to be done with parents who have children in the school and with the pastor, parish council and education board. I once spent a week consulting with a parish about family catechesis, and while staff, pastor, and people were ready to move in that direction, the education board refused to look honestly at their financial priorities, the pastor refused to make a strong statement, and I suspect the religious education director is still struggling with the problem, if he is still there.

An urban parish may require more pastoral family ministry than catechetical ministry, depending on the composition and location of the parish. There may also be greater financial problems in an urban or inner city parish than in other parishes. My experience has been, however, that a family program can be much less expensive to maintain than any other parish program, depending on how it is implemented. In any event, I think many of the principles already stated can be as valid for the urban as well as suburban or rural parishes. An urban parish can also look into the possibility of teaming up with other urban parishes or with a sister-parish in the suburbs to share personnel and programs.

The sharing of programs could be a marvelous learning experience for both types of parishes. Such an arrangement would require some serious teamwork between the staffs of the two parishes and some pre-catechesis in order to be workable. A shared program, particularly between an urban and suburban parish, might appropriately be designed around the idea of families ministering to one another, with participating families experiencing activities together a few times a year so that relationships between individual families can be established. It could give both groups of families an opportunity to become less parochial and develop a slightly more global awareness.

The urban parish will also need to be more keenly aware of needs of special families, such as families with one parent, and will want to adapt their programs and events to meet those needs. That kind of awareness and sensitivity, of course, all of us must have when we are developing family programs. The nuclear family is now a minority in our culture, and our programs must reflect these shifts and changes in societal reality.

Whatever your approach, wherever your parish is located, you will want to implement a program that relates to the specific needs of your people. The manner in which that is done will depend to a great extent on your own personality and philosophy of religious education as well as your ability to work with your parish staff and parishioners, and your sincere efforts to determine their needs and desires.

Maintaining a family program in a parish is not an easy job but it can be done and can be immensely rewarding to both you and your families. It is my hope that this case study of what was done at St. Joseph's and the suggestions for other approaches in other types of parishes will be an encouragement and support for what you, too, can do to develop family catechesis.

Most families want to have times of family sharing, but they have not come to grips with their calendars. They lack the skills to choose among several experiences they consider good for their children and themselves.

Chapter 4

Faith Sharing and Home Activities

Moving into the Heart of Family Catechesis

A family program runs the risk of becoming just another religious education program for which the family comes to the parish if it does not provide motivation for the family to share faith at home.

Generally, before families are involved in a family program, they do not engage in a great deal of deliberate faith sharing or even religious discussion at home. In my experience, young parents often come to pre-baptism sessions without any experience in reflecting with each other about their faith. Nor are those parents comfortable sharing their faith with their children.

Providing inspiration, encouragement, practical suggestions, and more encouragement to enable families to share at this intimate level of their lives is an essential objective of the director-catechist ministering to families. The confidence and the skills come slowly. Parents have a long, ingrained conditioning which tells them that only the priest, Sister or the classroom teacher can really teach religion. You not only have to change their thinking from "teaching" to "faith sharing," but also, you have to help them convince themselves that they can do that faith sharing best, because they have the greatest opportunities for this.

Be prepared to be disappointed in your efforts, because although you suggest numerous activities to families to facilitate their faith sharing, they will return time and again, not having attempted them and feeling guilty because they haven't.

I think there are two basic reasons to explain this behavior. First, they have calendar problems. They have not dealt with the forces which separate their families nor taken the time to determine what is most important and necessary for themselves. Failing to establish consciously chosen priorities, families will be tempted by an abundance of valuable (and some not so valuable) opportunities offered by Church and Society. The family can find itself over-involved, over-scheduled, and fragmented. Their home becomes a hotel of passing occupants.

Consequently, families need help, first and foremost, in setting priorities. You can challenge them at one of the first family gatherings that you have with them to commit themselves to family time together, and to believe that sharing faith together is possible for their family.

Most families want to have such time together, but have not come to grips with their calendars, or lack the skills to choose among several experiences they consider good for their children and themselves. Sit down and discuss the situation with them; this may reveal that Sissy really doesn't want to take part in Blue Birds anymore anyway, even though it has been a good experience. Or perhaps, the family will decide that five-year-old Tommy can learn to play hockey some other year. Maybe the family will decide to rearrange their television viewing, or to take more time for the family evening meal. Whatever the case, you can help families come to those decisions by asking critical questions in a manner that does not trigger guilt or anger. You cannot make the decisions for them; you can only help them to make their own.

A good format for helping families set some time for family faith sharing, once they decide to make it a priority, is in Lois Bock and Miji Working's book, *Happiness Is A Family Time Together* (Revell, 1975). The chapter entitled "Getting Started" includes family discussion on how to make special family times work, and a Family Growth Covenant for all members of the family to agree to and sign. The Covenant reads:

We the _____ family covenant to meet regularly for the purpose of knowing better one another and the will of God. Unless unusual circumstances prevent, we will meet each _____ day at _____ o'clock. The signatures below show our willingness to take part and make this time a helpful one for our family. Signed:

A covenant of this type is helpful for families.

Insecurity, fear of failure, and embarrassment are other reasons why parents are reluctant to try the suggestions that you provide for home experiences. To help them overcome these feelings takes time. As mentioned earlier, younger families will find it easier than those with older children, because the embarrassment is less acute. Providing the hesitant families with models and with initial, simple experiences are two other ways of helping them to move toward trying similar experiences in their own homes.

It might also be possible for you to match families, so that families who have a tradition of family faith sharing at home could meet with a family just beginning such experiences for an inter-family activity. This is more successful if the families live near one another. Encourage two or three families to plan family times together, whether they are experienced or not, simply because the support of other parents is helpful, and there is also greater possibility of the commitment to family time being lived out because of the commitment to other people besides one's own family.

Making your suggestions for family experi-

ences to the whole family sometimes is helpful. If the children find your description of the family experience interesting, they may request parents try it. You also have provided the parents with a mutual experience to which they can refer. This is a rather backwards approach, very much like the unspoken goal of many Catholic schools and religious education programs which hope that children will lead their parents to active participation in the Church.

You can also offer to go into homes and conduct one or two family sessions with the parents. This helps them to see that the activities are really uncomplicated and relatively easy. When you do this, you should plan the sessions ahead of time with the parents and enable them to take the leadership role, with your presence being mostly a reinforcement or assistance when they need it. Spend some time afterwards with the parents giving them positive reinforcement.

There are few, if any, family faith sharing experiences which fail, and as my mother always says, "Nothing succeeds like success." Point out their successes. Often, parents cannot imagine the very meaningful things that happen during these family times until they have experienced a few of them.

The best way to overcome parental feelings of inadequacy, however, has to do with the kinds of suggestions that you send home. I have seen many which are pure and simple cases of moving the classroom into the home. These are disastrous, because they structure the parents in an authoritarian role which does not facilitate faith sharing, but rather doctrinal input. Since not all parents are teachers, these suggestions immediately place an expectation on them that is unfair and increases their insecurity. The more simple and natural to family life the suggestions, the better they are and the easier they will be for families to use.

As a general rule, home suggestions should be simple, short, fun, natural, non-classroom, and include a food treat. Also suggest some home activities which happen spontaneously in the family and which, by your suggestion,

Emphasize that everyone in the family, parents included, must participate fully in the home activity.

---

parents begin to realize are opportunities to express their faith. These are the actions which constitute teachable moments.

In all honesty, I must confess that I am less concerned with whether families engage in the suggested home activities, and much more concerned with how they live the faith at home, answer their children's questions, listen to their children and to each other, take time to be with their children, and celebrate being family by simply enjoying one another.

Since many parents are unaware of the value of such aspects of family life which they consider "natural and what they would do anyway," providing activities which are equally natural helps them see the importance of what they have been doing all along. Then, as time goes on, the suggestions become an impetus and motivation for even more and better family faith sharing. The home activities and rituals which you suggest and share in your program provide the environment through which you can affirm parents in what they are already doing and help them do it even better.

Home suggestions therefore can take two forms: the spontaneous moments of faith sharing of which parents simply need to become aware, and the planned, special, ritual-type activities. For a beginning program, I would suggest the activities and rituals which appear unplanned to the family. They are the most likely to succeed with the least amount of preparation and effort and provide a sense of confidence for parents. The signing of the children before going to bed is one of those. Others which I have suggested and which have been used effectively with families are:

—Pray together as a family before going to bed.
—Take the family for a walk in the park, the woods, to the zoo, or to a farm. On the way home, engage them in conversation to point out things they saw that showed God's love in the world.
—Make it a point to speak to someone you don't know after celebration of Eucha-

rist on Sunday, or take time to chat with a friend. Your children will pick up that Eucharist is truly a banquet of love.
—Be prepared to say "I'm sorry" for your own mistakes. Remind the children to forgive those who are unkind to them.
—On one day each week for a month, plan and serve a family meal that costs no more than $2, with the realization that there are families in our city who must do this daily. Calculate the amount of money saved in a month and give the money to some organization engaged in acts of justice or mercy.
—Let your children share in some Christian act of your own, e.g., taking food to someone who is ill.
—Help your child review the good and not-so-good things s/he did each day. (This is the beginning of learning a personal examination of conscience.)
—Examine your own conscience to see what sort of example you set for your children: Do you talk unkindly about the neighbors? Cheat on traffic laws? Stress the importance of wealth and "getting up in the world"? Cheat your employer? Pray in front of your children? Joyfully celebrate liturgy? Enjoy the simple things of life? Help others?
—For one day keep track of all the opportunities that occur for religious discussion with your children. Do you make use of them?
—Respond as a family to another family in need, for example, fire victims.

When making some of these suggestions, however, don't do what I did once. I listed them all, plus several more, on a sheet of paper and said, "These are some good suggestions for you to try at home." The result: None of them were attempted because there were too many. Give one or two at a time, and ask parents to choose one or both to do for the month. Then suggest a few more the following month. The purpose of this type of suggestion is to help parents become aware of the many little things they are perhaps already doing which are valuable for their children's faith development.

Related to the natural and spontaneous type home suggestions is the need to discuss Christian attitudes and how they are transmitted to children by what is said and how it is said, by what is done and not done, through comments and attitudes toward life, people, Church. Parents need to be aware of how such seemingly insignificant remarks, tone of voice, actions, non-actions and attitudes, influence their families. I like to tell the following story to help parents' awareness. It is a story I heard from another DRE.

The teacher was having a terrible problem with Oscar who continuously took pencils from the other children's desks. At least once a week, Oscar had to empty his desk of all his collected pencils so the other children in the class could reclaim their pencils. In desperation, the teacher called Oscar's father in and told him of the problem. The father shook his head and said, "I just don't understand that at all; I certainly bring enough pencils home for him from the office."

Helping parents be cognizant of the many little things that they do and say that affect their children's faith growth is one of the family director's most important roles. Likewise helping them to recognize teachable moments, which often come at the most inopportune times, and encouraging them to take the time to respond to those moments is equally important. Those short moments of answering questions, listening, comforting, or simply giving attention are moments they can utilize for sharing faith with their families.

It is estimated that the three-year-old, for example, asks 390 questions a day. Each of those questions can be a teachable moment and many of them occasions for sharing faith.

The home activities or rituals which require special planning are more or less effective depending on the needs of your families. While I think the more informal, spontaneous faith sharing and family home rituals are the most

important in family life, many families want to have regularly planned home activities. If your needs assessment revealed this desire on the part of families, I would suggest your using one of the several published family activities booklets available today. I mentioned some of them previously; others are listed in the bibliography.

When using these, know the resource well so that you can recommend sections which are in keeping with the particular theme or topic that is being covered. Simply handing the book to parents is as futile as my listing all the home activity suggestions at once. Furthermore, you will want to pick and choose from the books, because like packaged programs, the suggestions sometimes need to be modified for your particular situation.

If you have the time, my stronger recommendation would be for you to have access to as many of the resources available today as possible and design activities that are best for your families. You will only be able to do that after you have come to know your families. Then the activities should be in keeping with their general personalities and family styles.

Emphasize that everyone in the family, parents included, must participate fully in the activity. What can tend to happen, if you don't stress the importance of total family involvement, is that parents often will ask the questions or give the directions to children and watch them perform the entire activity without ever personally joining in, consequently, still not sharing faith with their children.

I have also found that some families need me to "walk through" the activity or ritual with them rather than just handing them out or sending them in the mail. Sometimes I provide opportunities for a small group of parents to experience the activity as adults. Again, the modelling and experiencing give them a sense of security in leading it themselves when the time comes. This is especially true of parents who are just beginning involvement in a family program. As time goes on, you will have to do less of that type of nurturing and will be able, instead to provide more challenges for them.

Chapter 5

By Their Rites You Shall Know Them

The Importance of Rituals for Sharing Faith

Harvey Cox, in his book *Feast of Fools,* points out that human beings are by their very nature creatures who not only work and think but who sing, dance, pray, tell stories and celebrate. He calls us *homo festivus.* "No other creature we know of," he says, "relives the legends of his forefathers [sic], blows out candles on a birthday cake, or dresses up and pretends he/she is someone else. Human beings are natural ritualizers."

We seem to forget this or at best, do not give enough credit to the prominence ritual plays in our lives and to the need we all have for it.

Because ritual is an integral part of life, it is at the center of the Church's life. In the past we used to call them church or family devotions. Then we became aware that our rituals had become merely prescribed or mechanical procedures, formal structures without heart to be followed for religious obligation. They no longer were flowing out of our sense of community, our common experiences, our needs, our imagination, our sense of immediacy with our history.

Now we are at the point of developing a new level of appreciation and incorporation of ritual into our lives. That does not mean a return to rituals which became meaningless because of cultural changes, but rather it means the creative development of new rituals for a new age which express the lived experience today—rituals which help us reflect on both our sacred and our secular experiences and see them as one.

We need new rituals which will not only carry us through crises but which will also carry us through the repetitious and mundane. We need rituals which will intuitively and affectively communicate meaning to our spirits by means of story, symbol and action. We need rituals which enhance the meaning of special moments in our lives and open us to communicate the faith that is within.

In my opinion, ritual (the combination of myth, symbol and action) is the most effective catechetical method to use in the religious formation of families, keeping in mind our goal of growth and development in faith. Why? Because ritual is a community's fullest expression of itself—with its history-made-present and its movement or passage toward new stages of life as a result of the transformation effected within the ritual. Ritual speaks to the whole person and imparts a wholistic knowledge. (Western culture particularly equates knowledge with the head. Eastern culture, including the culture out of which springs our scriptures, has a much broader, more affective and relational understanding of "knowing." Western understanding of knowledge results in science; Eastern understanding of knowledge expresses itself in poetry.)

Words, classes, books, pictures alone cannot adequately communicate what is in the heart—and these media characterize our former catechetical approaches. Ritual with its elements of story, symbol and action characterizes a catechesis that reaches us and transforms us wholistically.

We are natural ritualizers. Our most ordinary, commonplace experiences are ritualistic: parties, parades, watching football, conventions, walking the dog, homecoming. Yet we seldom reflect on these as rituals which carry with them deeper meanings or convey truths about our lives.

Children, especially, live by rituals. Watch a child at play. Note the order, the predictability of the marbles game, the hopscotch, the rope jumping. The ritual of a child jumping rope is neither a mere repetitive diversion nor a conceptualized mode of instilling the values of patience, endurance, sharing and cooperation into the child. Yet, through the repetitive ritual experience of word, symbol, and action—"blue bells, cockle shells, eensy, eeny over"—these values, even though they are not perceived conceptually, are made present and effective.

Ritual accomplishes two things that are not conveyed better through any other method of catechesis. It conveys truth concretely rather than abstractly and it reactualizes or *real*-izes that truth *now*. To jump rope, there are rules not to be broken, and the truth here is that without patience, endurance, sharing and cooperation, the play is false or unreal.

In the realm of religious growth, we must recognize that there is no such thing as abstractions of faith. Community, God, love, hope, etc. as abstractions are quite unimportant. They are important only if they are actual. Their reality can be expressed best through symbols and creative play.

And ritual in a very real sense is creative play. Transactional analysts tell us that for religious experience and prayer to be internalized, the "adult" has to get the "parent" off the "child's" back. I think ritual can help that to happen. As W. H. Auden says, "Only in rites can we renounce our oddities and be truly entired."

Through ritual we are able to express the faith which is often difficult for us to verbal-

ize. Through ritual we enact what is in the heart. In short, ritual is the expression through myth, symbol and action of the faith and faith activities of individuals and communities, now and through history. Or as Gerard Pottebaum says in his marvelous little book *The Rites of People* (The Liturgical Conference): "Ritual is the dramatic form through which people in community make tangible in

---

The leader or presider of communal ritual is a model of cordiality, sincerity, festivity, and willingness to share one's personal faith.

---

symbol, gesture, word, and song what they have come to believe is the hidden meaning of their experience in relationship with the world, with others and with their God."

In the context of family catechesis, we speak of aiding families in the sharing of faith. I strongly believe that nothing accomplishes this as effectively as family and community ritual. Through ritual the family and community are able to express the faith that is within. Children can see it concretely, can appreciate both the faith expressed and the people revealing it, can grow from it and can likewise share their own faith concretely within the group. Thus they become not just learners who have to know certain things in order to belong to the community, as our religious education programs tend to make them, but sharers in the life and actions of that community.

Parents, at the same time, are not teaching, but are growing in the faith, expressing that faith, and their children are growing as a result of the communication of their parents' faith growth.

In ritual the community's story and action

merge and emerge. We remember and act in symbolic ways which bring tradition and our lives together. A celebration of the Passover Meal, for example, is neither a reminiscence of a fable about some angelic boogey man who slaughtered the bad guys and saved the good guys nor an abstract formula explaining the essence of God and God's cosmic plan. Rather it is a re-enactment of God's faithful

Not a learning that is a compilation of facts or memorized answers.

I am also speaking of a ritual that is responsive to people, perhaps an assumption that can easily be slipped into. Bringing together family catechesis and ritual can have a salutary effect on our ritualizing sensitivities. In designing rituals (a subject I will address in greater detail in the next chapter), we must see

---

By your rites they will know you, and by knowing you they will come to know your faith and have the freedom to express their own faith with you and with one another.

---

love made present here and now for all those celebrating and indeed in communion with all those who have preceded us in the Judean-Christian tradition. The movement from the Passover ritual celebrated by the Hebrews to the rite of Eucharist, first celebrated by Jesus and then by his followers as they remembered down through the ages, expresses our present-day belief in that faithful love continuing, and that we ourselves now experience. The story (the history) is ongoing in the symbol and action.

If our children are to know our faith and share in it, they must ritualize with us, for it is through ritual that the truth and truths of our faith are re-actualized and *real*-ized today. Ritual holds or embraces the whole of the content of our faith because each of us is there as believing persons.

The goal of ritual is not to educate *per se.* Consequently, no one comes to ritual intent on learning, nor do they go away from ritual enumerating what they have learned; but learning in fact does take place. I am speaking of a learning that happens as a result of experience reflected upon and integrated into life.

to it that they do provide moments for reflection, integration, and articulation.

Myth

Another word I might need to clarify is "story" or "myth." Story or myth in ritual conveys a truth concretely. The details of the story need not be true, but the message or reality it conveys is true. For example, the specifics of the story of George Washington's cutting down the cherry tree is probably not true, but the truth conveyed through that story is that honesty is an important virtue in the lives of Americans as modeled by our first president. Many of our stories in scripture must be understood similarly.

In our catechesis and rituals with families, we are presenting *the* story of our God's relationship with a covenant community, of a parish community, of a family community, of an individual's own journey in faith. This is the message we want to convey. Those of us in the business of religious education sometimes can get so caught up in the historical, formal, or literary interpretations of scripture, that we

> The joining of the sacred and secular in our lives is much needed today. People are desperately searching for spiritual renewal in bible study, prayer groups, and any number of specially designed programs of spiritual growth. We are passing by the natural and common experiences and symbols which reveal the holiness of life. In our search we step on the violet instead of lying on our stomachs to hear what it might be able to tell us.

greater psychological ease. In addition, parents find the technique a growing experience, since, in reality, a large percentage of children's stories are stories for adults because of the depth of meaning within them.

I suggest you obtain a list of all of the Newbery and Caldecott award-winning children's books and spend some summer or Christmas vacation enjoying them. These lists can be acquired through most public libraries. Some of the lists that I have seen also include the books that were runners up for the awards and are usually as good, and sometimes better than, the award-winning book.

Another very helpful reference for finding nonreligious literature for use in family rituals is *An Annotated Bibliography of Inexpensive Paperbacks for Religious Education: Preschool Through High School,* compiled by Dr. Robert J. Fitzsimmons (289 West Lane, Kensington, CT 06037). Dr. Fitzsimmons has divided the books according to age level and also according to topic, theme, title and author, and has included publishers' addresses as well.

Numerous tales have been written specifically for religious education use that are usable as myths: *The Giving Tree* by Shel Silverstein (Harper and Row), *The Way of the Wolf* by Martin Bell (Seabury), *Hope for the Flowers* by Trina Paulus (Paulist). *The Giving Tree* has also been made into a well-done film. Jack Miffleton has written some fine parabolic stories that are usable in a family setting. Most of his have been compiled into record sets and include a ready-made ritual which incorporates the story, song and activity. These sometimes have to be modified since they are usually child-oriented.

The Parables is a filmstrip series by Ed and Maureen Curley (Twenty-Third Publications), which retells the parables of Jesus in modern situations. These filmstrips, which themselves might be incorporated as the story element in your ritual, exemplify the nature of myth or story—the details can change, but the truth conveyed remains.

Storytelling is much more effective than story reading, whether the story be your own

fail to tell the story. I know I can and have.

I learned over my eight years of working with families that the truth of the message is conveyed much more effectively when the story is told or when it is dramatized, danced, mimed or sung, than when it is read and then dissected.

Using a nonreligious story, or a story by a contemporary author which expresses the same truth as a scripture passage is also effective. Children's literature has volumes of such stories. The use of these stories is particularly palatable to children; they listen more carefully and can make the association between the story, the scripture message and real life with or someone else's. Telling the story requires that something of yourself is put into it. At the same time, one cannot tell a story without sharing faith. Facial expression, inflections of the voice, eye contact, body movements—all these communicate more of what is within us that is meaningful to us than the mere words of the story. Facial expression alone conveys 40% of whatever we are trying to communicate—or not communicate.

Parents today are concerned that their children know bible stories. I get numerous inquiries wondering which of the many children's bibles on the market today is the best. There are several that are good, but I always recommend that parents *tell* bible stories to their children. They will communicate their faith more effectively that way than by spending the money for a bible. Moreover, their children will be more appreciative of the time spent with them, and of the closeness that will be experienced during the storytelling.

One cannot tell children a story without sitting close to them. In family workshops, there is a natural migration to get as close as possible to the storyteller. Even adults move closer, and it is not uncommon when I am telling a story to have three children on my lap, two over my shoulders and at least one next to me, who has wrapped my arms around herself. Because I am only five feet tall and sitting on the floor, in a situation like that, I have to do an awful lot with my voice and my eyes—just in case someone can see my eyes.

We cannot tell a story without telling something about ourselves, and when one person risks telling something about him/herself, others take courage to risk similarly. We may be telling a story from scripture, but through the telling we are also telling a story about ourselves, our family, our community, our traditions. It is inevitable. It cannot be helped.

For a good intergenerational experience sometime, invite senior citizens from the parish in to tell the story of how they celebrated Christmas as children. They will tell much more than the factual story; they will share a faith of such depth and sincerity that parents will be teary-eyed, and wide-eyed children will

be requesting parts of the story to be repeated and will ask questions. It is a moving experience, and one that can spark families to start or enrich their own Christmas traditions in an attempt to imitate the traditions shared by the seniors.

The film is a good storyteller, too. Numerous good religious films are out today, and also some superb films that are not strictly religious. Taking some time to go to your public library to preview their collection can be a valuable and often enjoyable way to spend what might be otherwise a gloomy day in the office.

Using drama to tell the story takes more time and effort, but is extremely effective, and involves the participants to a greater extent. We have used drama to tell the story of John the Baptizer, to express the message of the Mystical Body, of Advent, and the story of the Ten Lepers. At a Family Eucharistic Liturgy, we once used a dramatization of the story of the "Selfish Giant" from the book *The Happy Prince* by Oscar Wilde (Puffin Books) to help ritualize the message of growth toward unity.

One summer we produced an eight-millimeter film of the Life of Christ with child actors of all ages, and parent directors, producers, photographers, film editors, music directors, and consultants. A lot of work was involved and the film has only been shown once; but the experience of putting it all together and the excitement of opening night were worth the time and energy.

Poetry as a message-maker also has numerous possibilities. It, like any story or myth, must be well read or recited, preferably recited or proclaimed. We tend to shy away from poetry, because we fear that people will not understand it. Or if we use poetry, we are tempted to interpret it. But like scripture or any art, when used as message-carrier, poetry must be allowed to be interpreted by the listener for the listener, or it ceases to be real myth and becomes instead the vehicle for the study of that particular art piece or occasion for a didactic sermon.

Songs, too, both religious and secular can be storytellers. The ballads of old and of today are written precisely to do that. Combining instrumental music with story or poetry is also extremely effective, to enhance the mood as an aid to communicating the message.

An absolute when re-telling a myth is this: never, never explain the meaning of the myth. A good myth does not need explanation; it speaks for itself because it speaks to individuals where they are. What makes myth (and

no one's application of the myth to his/her life is to be disputed; and no one's understanding of the myth is to be applied to another person's life.

The language style of faith-sharing is characterized by abundant use of the first-person singular pronouns. "I hear. . . ," "I think God is asking me to . . ." "When I listened to the story, I felt . . ."

At a ritual children are not just learners who have to know certain things in order to belong to the community, but they are sharers in the life and actions of that community.

---

ritual) so powerful for individuals is that they provide a format which captures the imagination and stirs the desire in individuals to search out the meaning within the story as it relates to their own experience and challenges them to seek new and deeper ways of living their response to the truth conveyed.

Explaining the myth is commensurate to a poet explaining the meaning of his/her poem before reciting it. The danger in explaining the meaning of a myth is that you explain what it means to you, which is not necessarily what it means or ought to mean for others. Each of us responds to myth according to our own self awareness and our readiness to be converted. Explication does violence to the myth, and to the listeners. It is not unlike answering questions before they are asked. Furthermore, it turns a ritual experience into a classroom experience in which there is the expectation that something very specific must be learned from the story. Such action destroys the purpose of both myth-making and ritual-making.

This is not to say that participants cannot be asked to share what the myth says to them about their own lives. Indeed, such sharing is to be encouraged. The underlying rule is that

Although I as leader sometimes refrain from talking during this faith-sharing time, lest my understanding becomes the "authoritative" one, I also think clearly modeling the individuality of faith-sharing style is valuable.

I prefer to allow the sharing to take place within the circle of the individual family. Providing this opportunity for sharing within families helps family members appreciate one another. The experience is affirming for both parents and children. Many parents are amazed at their children's depth of faith and understanding. And, of course, children have a rare insight into their parents' faith, and can learn that faith involves doubt, questioning, and weakness, as well as generosity, strength, and perseverance.

Some family members may get nothing out of the myth, and that is all right, too. It is important to give people the freedom and the permission to be totally untouched by the myth sometimes.

Symbol

Symbol is an element of ritual. Myths are powerful symbols that take place in the imagination. Other symbols incorporated into the ritual are sensuously operative, i.e., they can be touched, smelled, felt, held, tasted, seen, listened to, played with. We know the importance of utilizing the senses in the traditional education process; yet somehow, in our worship and praying we have not yet utilized effectively even our existing ecclesial symbols, much less the natural cultural symbols which can speak just as loudly of our relationship to the transcendent.

Our lives are filled with sensuous objects capable of becoming symbols of the meaning we find in our experiences and existence. Christmas is not Christmas without Christmas trees; Easter needs decorated eggs; birthdays need cakes; autumn in most sections of the country needs multicolored leaves; Halloween gives us the opportunity to dress up and pretend we are our hero or heroine for a while.

Symbols become for us what they signify, that's how powerful they are. Did you ever try to celebrate Thanksgiving without turkey? If you have children who have had the experience of Thanksgiving with turkey, it is nearly impossible for them to imagine the day without the bird.

Ask a child about a photo, and the response will reveal that for the child the photo is indeed the presence of that person, "That's my Uncle Sam." Grandparents do the same thing with photos of grandchildren. The piece of paper with an image on it is seldom "a picture of my grandchild," rather, "This *is* my grandchild."

And it is not only children and grandparents for whom symbols are what they say they are. In our family, we have the custom, which I assume came to this country with our ancestors, of having a special stewed onion dish on Christmas Eve. For me, Christmas Eve always meant crying over peeling what seemed like hundreds of onions, then smelling them cook all day, and finally having to eat them. I never liked them, and my mother knew that; but everyone had to have some every year.

Not long ago, I arrived home on Christmas Eve afternoon, walked into the house, sniffed, and noticed a definite absence of stewing onions. I barely said hello before I asked, "Where are the onions?" My mother looked at me in a hurt sort of way and said, "I know you don't like them, so I didn't make any this year."

"But Mom," I said, "it's not Christmas Eve without onions." So we rolled up our sleeves and began peeling, crying, and cooking onions.

For others in my family, other special Christmas Eve symbols signify the day. For some it is the special square noodles, the fried codfish that has been dried and salted, and then soaked all week, or the special fried bread with raisins. For my father, it's delivering presents to my parents' many godchildren. For anyone not in our family circle, each of these symbols could have an entirely different meaning. I learned in working with Indians in Northern Wisconsin, for example, that fried bread has nothing to do with Christmas for them; but I was told that, if I placed a piece of

---

No one comes to ritual intent on learning, nor do they go away from ritual enumerating what they have learned; but learning does take place.

---

it taken from a wedding celebration under my pillow, I would dream of a handsome young man and be married within a year. I didn't try it, so I don't know if the symbol is indeed that powerful.

The point of my story, however, is that symbols function on two levels of meaning. A symbol has an objective, conventional or natural meaning, so that for those not of the Ojibway Indian culture or the Neopolitan ancestry, fried bread might be simply fried bread, square noodles are square noodles and stewed onions are stewed onions. A symbol also has a subjective or affective meaning within which there is the possibility for several different emotions or conditions which enable the symbol to signify more than it communicates on the objective level.

Symbols must function on the two levels of meaning to have their full impact. These two levels of meaning open boundless possibilities for the use of symbols. Utilizing the very natural symbols of everyday life—leaves, apples, flowers, rocks, butterflies, eggs, the sun, the moon, salt, wood—in creative ways not only helps people relate to the commonplace in their lives, but also aids in the wedding of the sacred and the secular.

That joining of sacred and secular in our lives is much needed today. People are desperately searching for spiritual renewal in bible study, prayer groups, and any number of specially designed programs of spiritual growth and are passing by the natural and common experiences and symbols which reveal the holiness of life. In our search we step on the violet instead of lying on our stomachs to hear

---

In designing rituals, we must see to it that they provide moments for reflection, integration, and articulation.

---

what it might be able to tell us.

Besides having two levels of meaning, symbols perform two functions in ritual: they invite us to take meaning from them and they call us to take a stand. The second function follows the first. Once we have discovered a meaning for ourselves in the symbol, once we have come face to face with the depth of our experiences, we are compelled to take a stand with regard to the meaning. Investing the symbol with meaning for ourselves and assuming a stance is inevitably followed by action based on that incorporation of the symbol into ourselves.

One PFL ritual that we had was a healing service in which families were encouraged to bring relatives, neighbors and friends who were ill. During the ritual we were invited to pray over them and join in anointing them. One family brought a neighboring family, who had an 11-year-old hydrocephalic child to the healing service. The decision to do this was a difficult one for the family, and much parental discussion and family preparation took place before the parents finally brought the children to meet the child, who was really rather monstrous looking. Once at the service, the PFL family sat around the child, who was carried in and laid on a special cot we provided for him. They prayed over him and laid hands on him and anointed him. It was a moving experience for both families and a healing experience for the mothers of both families. But the situation which followed the service was even more moving and emphasizes the role that symbol can play in our lives.

At the conclusion of the ritual, a 15-year-old girl approached me inquiring about the child on the cot. After I explained his physical situation, she asked if he could hear. Not being sure, I suggested that we ask his mother. When the mother informed the girl that she thought he could hear and seemed to enjoy soft radio music, the 15-year-old asked if it would be all right with the parents if she would come over periodically and play her guitar and sing for him, because she did not live far away.

Needless to say, the symbols of that ritual had effected what they spoke that night. Healings took place in ways that we never expected. That is the beauty of the wonder and surprise that ritual and symbols hold out for us, if we allow them to find meaning in ourselves and then act on those meanings as the young girl did.

Perhaps one reason we fill our processes of

education with so much verbiage is our desire to control what's happening. We feel safe when we control and can predict what will happen and what will supposedly be understood. To shift the emphasis from words to symbols becomes risky. Someone might miss what they are supposed to catch, someone might make a different interpretation than we

that would gather the experience of the day and lift them in prayer including a breaking and sharing of bread and wine to symbolize the friendship of the group.

At the December PFL Family Workshop, Kathie, the new family catechist in the parish, gave each family a paper bag and a piece of paper for each family member which said: "I

A good myth, symbol, or ritual action does not require explanation. It speaks for itself and it speaks to the individual participants according to their own self-awareness and readiness to be converted.

---

had planned. But that is the joy and power of symbol and ritual. It is creative. We throw possibilities out to people, and some of them may catch them and some may not. That's the nature of catechesis based on the Gospel. It invites the free response: "Let the one who has ears to hear, hear; the one who has eyes to see, see."

For those who do, the meanings they catch will make a difference in their lives. They will begin seeing the world and their relationships in the world in a new light. The circus will begin to have as much religious significance as the Advent wreath. The naming of the new baby will be as holy a responsibility as the child's Baptism. The teachable moment will be recognized and utilized because we have helped families discover the value of the ordinary and concrete in the life of faith.

It does happen. As I was writing this chapter, a family who had been in PFL for several years called explaining that their family and five other families were getting together for a New Year's Eve Day of cross-country skiing and sledding. They were looking forward to a day to enjoy the beauties of winter and friendship and asked if I could join them for dinner and lead a special ritual to cap off that day. They explained that they wanted something

(name) have this Christmas wish for my family in the coming year . . . To be shared New Year's Eve at a Prayer-Party." The papers were filled in at the workshop and placed in the bag which was to be put under the Christmas tree unopened until New Year's Eve.

The PFL families arranged for their non-PFL friends to have papers and bags at the New Year's Eve ritual and directed me to be sure to include the sharing of the Family Wish Bags into the ritual for that night. They knew what they wanted the ritual to express.

The day was deliberately planned. I could see that the years of ritualizing with them were meaningful for them. The association between the secular and sacred was realized, their experiences were making sense because they felt comfortable ritualizing them, they were capitalizing on teachable moments for their children, and sharing faith with them. Furthermore, it was edifying to me to witness suburban parents celebrating New Year's Eve with their families. By their rites they came to know themselves, share themselves and express that which they wanted to become.

The ritual was simple, beginning with the families sharing the experiences of the day with me and with one another while I casually began setting the environment. In other words, they told their story. The room where the ritual took place had a marvelous fire burning in the fireplace. On a small coffee-table, we placed a large menorah, a loaf of bread and a carafe of wine. Against the base of the menorah, I leaned a stone replica of the Aztec sun calendar which I had brought with me. As I put it in place, someone asked what it was and we had some discussion of it, of the Aztec sun worship, and I tied it into the understanding of Sunday being the day of the sun and Hanukkah and Christmas being festivals of light.

Since that evening was the beginning of the last day of Hanukkah, we began the ritual proper with a lighting of the Festival Lights, praying the Jewish blessing as each family lit one of the candles. When the last candle was lit, we turned on a record of Richard Strauss' "Also Sprach Zarathustra" and quietly allowed the candlelight and the intensity of the introduction to the musical arrangement to fill our beings for a few minutes. As the music continued softly in the background, we listened to a reading from *Isaiah* (9:1, 5; 60:1, 19-20).

Our response to the reading was "Lord, Today" by the Dameans, which led us to pray: *Lord, our God, we ask you to be with us tonight as we celebrate a new beginning in the light of your son, a new beginning as the rising sun is the beginning of a new day. Be with us as we celebrate the beginning of a new year and a new beginning for each of us here, surrounded by those we love and the light of Christ. We pray you stay near us as we live this new beginning through the new year.*

We then opened the Wish Bags, each person sharing his or her wish for the family. I, too, shared my wish for each family. We listened to "Sabbath Prayer" from "Fiddler on the Roof," and moved into a breaking and sharing of bread and wine. The bread was broken by the host couple into six portions, one for each family present, and given to each couple to break and share within their families. The wine was also passed by the host family to each of the other families. We prayed a final prayer, sang a rousing "Amen,

Alleluia," shared a sign of peace for the New Year with one another and concluded with singing, dancing and clapping Peter Yarrow's "Weave Me the Sunshine."

I did not stay until midnight, but left the families with the suggestion that everyone go a little crazy at 12 o'clock, and maybe pop popcorn to symbolize the old bursting into newness.

I don't know if the symbol of light carried

Many parents are amazed at their children's depth of faith and understanding. And, of course, children have a rare insight into their parents' faith.

---

the same meaning for each of those 30 people that it did for me. Listening to the sharing of family wishes, observing the facial expressions, the words used and the spontaneous responses of individuals during the ritual lead me to believe that, indeed, meaning was derived from the symbol and ritual by all present to a greater or lesser degree. Parents told me later that they were hoping for a good religious experience for their children, yet found it to be a powerful experience for themselves as well. That is the beauty of using ritual in family catechesis. It is the one method which can reach all people in the program at each one's own level and not just the children. I too was moved by the ritual, because the spontaneity of the group and their participation added a spirit to the celebration which could only be experienced there and could not be imagined while I was designing it.

Response after the ritual also reminded me that effective rituals tend to become traditional. Dolores Curran says, "*Once* is a tradition for children." She is correct, and it is also true of adults when a ritual is particularly meaningful. Before I left those families that night, the children were already talking about next year's New Year's Eve and ritual. And as I walked out the door, one of the families informed me, "Next year's ritual will be at our house. We're not from this parish but we'll see that you get our address."

Good ritual with its use of symbol lingers in the memory; and in lingering, it allows us to revel in its meaning long after it is over.

Symbol is also cumulative. Our consciousness once sensitized keeps finding new significance and new interpretations as our lives continue to open up before us and we encounter the symbol in other contexts. Candlelight, the music and songs, paper bags, bread and wine, popcorn, and New Year's Eve can never have the same limited meanings they had for us before we celebrated that special New Year's Eve ritual.

Symbol, as myth, is self-explanatory. In using symbol as in using myth, do not explain it. Let it speak for itself. Let it be missed by some. Let it be interpreted in various ways and let people share what it means to them personally.

With the exception of the one unknown symbol, the Aztec sun calendar, all the other symbols were easily recognizable on their objective level of meaning. In this particular ritual, I did allow time for sharing of the sun calendar's meaning on its objective level; but this explanation was in response to a spontaneous inquiry. It was part of my story leading the participants into their stories and setting the mood and direction for the ritual itself. Until the Aztec calendar was used in this particular New Year's Eve ritual, it was not a symbol for the families—it was merely an object. Now, because it became surrounded with a concrete experience, it has symbolic meaning. Or to be more accurate, I should say it *might* have symbolic meaning for *some* of the participants. For the meaning of a symbol on its affective level cannot be forced, nor univocally interpreted.

Don't worry about those who might miss the significance of the symbol. In allowing the freedom to find meaning or not find meaning,

there is growth. We plant the seeds; the harvesting might occur at another time with other persons.

Ritual Action

Paul has written in one of his letters to an early church community, "Our bodies are temples of the Holy Spirit." Through our bodies we enact what is in the heart. In ritual, if the myth has conveyed a truth concretely to us and we experience symbolic meaning which calls us to take a stand, the natural flow is to act out in some physical way the deepened meaning, the renewed faith, the surprise or wonder of the moment.

For most American Catholics a free or large physical response is difficult to do, perhaps because we have been told so often that even though our bodies are temples of the Lord, the best room in the temple is from the neck up and that's really where the Spirit dwells. The rest we are not so positive about. We treat them as empty rooms which we rarely enter and seldom use in moments of ritual worship.

Gesture has always been part of ritual, basically however in the form of the way the celebrant held his arms and hands and genuflected.

Those are not the ritual actions I refer to here. Ritual action, as I understand it, is more. It is also the spontaneous action that comes from being called to take a stand. Both the structured gesture and the spontaneous action can happen within a particular ritual, or the latter might follow the ritual itself. In the New Year's Eve ritual described previously, we had several planned ritual actions. We lit candles, we shared wishes, we broke and ate bread, we drank wine and we danced. Without those actions, the ritual would have been a very dry recitation of words around some candles previously lit by someone. There were also some spontaneous actions within that ritual. The sharing of wishes from one family to another, the swaying to music, the tears, the hugs and kisses, and even the sign language exchanged between a deaf child and

> Any space can be used for ritual. It does not always have to be a designated sacred space such as the church or chapel. In fact, people and events make a space sacred.

his parents.

Although ritual is not fundamentally spontaneous, time and space should always be allowed for the surprising to take place; because ritual in a sense, inserts a new dimension to our present situation. If the ritual does, in fact, speak to the hearts of the ritualizers, then wonder, awe and surprise will be expressed sometimes verbally, sometimes in a physical response. Then you will know that the ritual is working. You will feel it.

Ritual action also adds the celebrative note to ritual. It may be as simple as exchanging apples with one another or as complex as a dance or group mime. But it is absolutely necessary because rituals must celebrate an experience. Rituals which are not celebrations are like the "old maids" at the bottom of the popcorn popper—they sizzle but they don't pop.

In short, rituals cannot be called rituals without ritual action. And the ritual action we employ can be anything at all which helps us *enact* what is in the *heart*. When performing a ritual action, whether it is simple or complex, not a word is spoken by the leader. Before or after the action, but not during the action. The action speaks for itself.

Ritual is more a sensuous and affective experience than it is a rational one. It is difficult to define or to describe it. Ritual must be *experienced;* it must be celebrated. While it cannot be defined easily or described, we almost always know it when we encounter it. When it is celebrated, there is interaction between two or more persons and the conscious attempt to look toward the transcendent in the hope that the Divine will be manifest anew in the present circumstances of life.

Ritual is celebrated *in the faith* that the Spirit will become present to us. It is that faith which families share in ritual. If and when that Divine disclosure is experienced, that,

too, is shared and celebrated. The mundane is broken through and we are changed.

Although I have just used hundreds of words to try to define the elements and components of ritual, in the final analysis, ritual is an art that each of us leaders of family programs must develop and cultivate. It is our vocation as leaders to provide ritual experiences which transform us and those with whom we serve. The rituals we celebrate with them will challenge them to serve the Lord willingly with their minds, lovingly with impassioned hearts and creatively with artistic abandon.

Ritual making is everyone's art. Therefore, our rituals at the parish center must be simple yet poignant so that families experiencing them will feel free and capable of trying their own rituals at home. If they are complex and not expressions of their lived situation, families will never feel able or desirous to ritualize the special events of their lives.

We can help families become aware of the family occasions that can be very simply yet significantly celebrated at home: birth, the naming of a baby, spring cleaning, yard raking, the first date, endings, beginnings, death as well as birthdays, anniversaries, and the ecclesiastical seasons. Doing this helps parents recognize teachable moments on which they can capitalize.

Once parents have created a few rituals, children will want to take over the ritual making for the family. Once your families begin experiencing success with ritualizing at home, encourage them to share their ritual with other families. Your encouragement will also be affirmation for them and excite them about their own giftedness.

Using ritual in family catechesis also can help us capitalize on what are customary secular rituals and help families enjoy a sense of holiness, of sacredness in seemingly profane rituals. To quote Gerard Pottebaum again:

"People come in touch with the sacred by discovering the holiness of the profane. We express this discovery—we make holiness tangible—through the dramatic art of ritual making. In this creative action, we come to enjoy a new spirit. We come to realize an even greater discovery, the joy of our lives: that we ourselves are the tangible expression of a Holy Spirit. That is something to parade through town about."

An example of how this can be done is Halloween. Generally, we have come to view Halloween as a "purely secular" celebration, designed basically for children. True, the holiday had a strikingly religious origin, but we are unrealistic to think that that tradition can be restored in all of its pristine innocence. Our culture does not warrant any such hope. We are a different people at a different time. As a Church though we can capitalize on what has become a customary secular ritual and help families enjoy a sense of the sacred in this seemingly profane ritual. If we could send the goblins and witches, the Spider Men and Draculas, the rabbits and princesses of our parish into the streets on Halloween with just a morsel of that realization, then they would indeed have something to parade through town about, and the materialistic treats offered by the elders of the community would have more than sugarcoated significance.

We have attempted to provide this sort of ritual experience in our parish. Although it was child-centered and does not serve as an example of ideal family ritualizing, our efforts were supportive of family needs and invited their participation. Two years ago we offered a Halloween afternoon liturgy for children and their parents, inviting children to come dressed in their masks and costumes. This year the children informed us that that liturgy was a tradition! This year a fairly large number of senior citizens attended the special Halloween liturgy. Likewise, this year, some parents came dressed in costumes and high school people provided mime as part of the liturgy. Some fathers arranged to leave work early to be with their families.

The format of the liturgy was simple. The sanctuary was decorated with dried weeds, cornstalks, pumpkins, jack-o-lanterns and candles; an autumn leaf mobile hung off center above the altar. We began with a rousing rendition of "When The Saints Come Marching In," followed by readings from *Colossians* 3:12-17 and *Mark* 10:13-16. In response between the readings, we sang and mimed Jack Miffleton's "I've Got a Hello" led by high school mimists, complete with white faces.

The pastor then engaged in an informal dialogue with the children about who they were pretending to be, what they were going to do on this night, and what struck them about the readings. Fortunately for the pastor's plan, one of the children stated that she really liked the section of the Gospel that depicted Jesus blessing and hugging little children. The conclusion of this dialogue was the announcement of a special treat that the pastor had for each child—a treat that had been given to him, that he would share with them: his individual blessing for each of them that they would have a safe and happy Halloween.

The next few minutes bordered on disorder with the pastor worming his way through wriggling children, some of whom unabashedly announced that he had passed them by, some who shamelessly pushed their way ahead of others, and several who came running down the aisle towing moms and dads for security. By the time we had sung "He's Got . . . everything from the Whole World to witches, goblins, monsters, bats, supermen, superwomen and disco-dancers in His Hands," the pastor had personally touched and blessed every one of nearly 200 children. All were then invited to share the hug and blessing of Jesus' peace with one another.

The ritual moved into the Liturgy of the Eucharist. After communion, all once again followed the mimists' gestures for "His Banner Over Me Is Love." The pastor wished everyone a Happy Halloween, lots of good treats, and requested that the children not play too many tricks, but rather remember to repay the treats they receive with thanks. All were sent on their way filled with excitement because dusk had settled in upon us without our noticing, and the aura of Halloween's spookiness had begun.

This attempt on our part to wed the secular and the sacred through creative ritual has many possibilities. The ritualization, of course, does not have to be annexed to the Eucharistic liturgy. The possibilities for non-Eucharistic rituals are boundless. Similarly, ritual need not be couched in so much traditional praying. The one thing ritual ought to help us do is recognize prayer in the ordinary; that God can be encountered while playing in leaves or appreciating a mountain or a work of art or a jackpine. We learn to find Christ the Clown at the circus or in a parade and, most of all, to recognize the Christ in ourselves and in our neighbors.

The ritualizing of Halloween suggests similar possibilities for the ritualizing of other so-called secular or profane holidays: July 4, Labor Day, President's Day, Election Day, the arrival of the circus in town, the city's annual Raspberry, Pickle, Ollie Olson or Rutabaga Festival, even the celebration of Homecoming or the opening of the class play.

There need not be a struggle to reveal the holiness entwined in our secular experience and rituals if we help families to do what ritual does so well—encounter the Lord. Seeing all of ritual, sacred or secular, as a means whereby we recognize and respond to the Spirit always within us, is the beginning of the easing of that struggle. As family catechists, we have a duty to help families toward that realization.

Ritual is also the method by which an integration of parish ministries can take place. Ritual, sacramental and non-sacramental, can be a means of simply ministering in the Church. In ritual we have a richness we have only begun to explore. As we do investigate the many possibilities for the use of ritual in our education as well as worship, perhaps the statement "By their rites you shall know them," will become less trite and more than mere rhetoric, but in fact a reality in the life of the Christian community.

We need make much better use of our rich liturgical heritage to serve the total parish life, worship, education, and social service. For too long the liturgist and the educator have been scorpions on each other's backs. We need to focus our energies in the one area which is so much a part of us, our ritual. If we did, we would worship better, educate better, and serve better than we are by fragmenting our resources into the One Rite (Mass), the Many Words (education), and the Christian Band Aids, (social service), often failing to see the relation between them. To educate is to educate for life. To ritualize is to capture life experiences and make them opportunities for encountering the Lord. To encounter the Lord is to serve. And it goes on. . . .

There is much more that could be said about how to go about creating and designing effective rituals. Setting the environment, utilizing space well, developing a sense of timing equivalent to the timing required for dramatic production, and organizing the structure are all important aspects of creating rituals. But at best I share with you only how I have done those things in the environment available to me. I don't think the ability to ritualize is primarily something that can be learned. The ability comes out of a comfort with your environment and an understanding and love of the people with whom you work. It comes from being what Matthew Fox calls a *symbolic thinker* rather than a *literal thinker*.

The best final advice I can give regarding the creation of rituals is to value them as growthful experiences of faith and not as techniques of programming. If you are not comfortable with or willing to or desirous of ritualizing your life experiences with your close friends and your own family, you may not be ready to ritualize with the families you serve.

The leader or presider of communal ritual models cordiality, sincerity, festivity, willingness to share his/her personal faith. By your rites they shall know you, and by knowing you they will come to know your faith and have the freedom to express their own faith with you and with one another. Together you will come to know the Lord who is the source and extension of that faith, and will be able to share that faith with the next generation.

Chapter 6

Ritual-Making with Families

Some Practical Advice from Experience

When my sister was married, the reception which followed her wedding was one of those marvelous large Italian extravaganzas (we Italians tend to do things in a big way or not at all when it comes to celebrations). Somewhere between the fourth course and dessert, my father stood up to call for a toast. The clinking of knives on glasses silenced the 200 guests. My father stood, wine glass raised high, pausing just long enough and then in his strong baritone sang:

Good-bye little darling we're parting,
Parting don't always mean good-bye.
You found someone new,
And he'll be good to you
Good-bye little darling, good-bye.

Good-bye little darling, I'll miss you
Just like the stars will miss the sky.
Though we'll be apart
You'll always have my heart
Good-bye, little darling, good-bye.

Finishing his song two verses before he really wanted to because my sister was crying and the groom was visibly nervous, my father drained his wine glass and watched as his guests did the same. Then he went over and kissed the bride, shook hands with and hugged the groom while he whispered something in his ear. Then he called for the cutting of the wedding cake.

As I reflect back on this incident, I realize that my father had just created and led us all through a perfectly structured ritual. He had

never studied ritual, but ritual had always been a part of his own family life. Consequently it had been an important part of our family life. It came natural to him; it's natural to me.

That's the way ritual making is cultivated in each of us—we learn it by participating in it. To move from being participant to being creator or presider at a ritual requires what my father exemplified at my sister's wedding: a sense of timing and of dramatic action, an awareness of the story (history made present in the now) being celebrated, and a willingness to express the feeling and faith of the moment with those others present.

The elements of ritual: myth (story), symbol, and action comprise a natural structural pattern or movement. The transition from one element of ritual to the other is not totally distinct as individual steps. Rather they flow into each other, and one becomes an extension of the other and enhances it.

Mood is important to the effectiveness of the ritual; it provides a quality of buoyancy to the essential elements. In ritualizing with families, one of the first steps is to establish the mood, to ready people to enter into the ritual. Mood is established in part by tending to the environment where the ritual will take place. How can you best use the space or spaces in which the ritual will take place? What will be the background for the ritual—what colors, what objects, what activity, what positioning of chairs, what sounds or music, etc.?

This setting of mood can also be done with some simple, but brief, dialoguing with families. Families are coming to ritual from various pleasant or unpleasant situations. There may have been a family argument around the dinner table, a quiet study time, or an exuberant family play time. The mood-setting aspect of the ritual structure must help families move from the past environmental situation to the present, if the ritual is to have its full impact upon them and if they are going to be present to it.

When you use the dialogical method to focus attention before moving into the story, be cautious of lapsing into didacticism—a teaching posture. Didacticism sets a classroom learning, teacher/student mood which will easily promote passive response and presence. The purpose of your initial conversational dialoguing with the family members is to gather or to focus attention, to bring together not only physically but mentally the participants into a mood conducive for ritualizing together.

The mood continues to be developed by the story (myth) you bring to share. The story helps us to move from where we were to the central point of where we are now, and where we may be led, given openness to the revelation of the story.

Good ritual, like drama, draws people into itself; and families, especially children, will be responsive. The Spirit is moving. Therefore, another aspect of ritual which the presiding ritualizer works with, not against, is its potential for surprise. You may have your ritual carefully planned and structured on paper or in your mind; but you must remain flexible to what is said and what happens. You listen or attend and are prepared to change pace, follow the mood, expand your symbolism or story, and act responsively. Rituals are created in part while they are being enacted. Immediacy is the heart of ritual, which explains why it is such a powerful medium for effective catechesis. It is faith happening here and now.

I begin the design of a ritual by asking, "What do we want to celebrate? How can we best express it—through which specific stories, symbols and actions?" Then, the ritual completed, I ask, "Did it work? Was it effec-tive and meaningful for those ritualizing?" I often can determine this by simply watching the participants and talking with them afterwards. I observe if there is a change in mood in participants from the time that the ritual began until its conclusion.

A less subjective aid in evaluating the effectiveness of ritual has been developed by Paul D. Jones, S.J. in his book *Rediscovering Ritual* (Newman Press, 1973). He asks four questions about ritual to help determine its effectiveness and success. I ask the questions both while I am creating a ritual and when I am a participant or leader in ritual, as well as afterwards to help me in my evaluation to determine the ritual's success. These questions are exactly what families spontaneously address in their own way when commenting on a ritual.

The first question has to do with time and timing:

Does the ritual lead participants into the dimensions of timelessness and free them from the standard getting-the-job-over-with attitude that characterizes most American experiences?

Ritual might be described as "wasting time with the Lord." A good ritual envelops us so that we forget what we came from, rise above it and are changed. Even if families approach ritual with a "let's-get-it-over" attitude, a good ritual will lift them above themselves into that sense of timelessness or immediacy. The finest compliment you can receive after a family ritual is, "The time seemed to go so fast."

I suggest you plan your ritual with a flexible concluding time. In that way, you allow for that good sense of "wasting time" or timelessness to happen. I schedule family workshops for one and one half hours and plan my rituals to last half that time (if all were to go as proposed). That way, I allow time for whatever might happen within the ritual to be spontaneously followed up. And I also bracket ample enough time so that the participants —particularly the adults—can be present and attentive without worrying about obligations and engagements that follow the time saved for "wasting with the Lord."

The second question deals with the symbolic event or symbols and action of the ritual:

Does ritual action become sacred and revelatory or is it characterized by elements of everydayness, routineness, impersonalism or obligation?

The symbols used in ritual must help people to experience both the sacredness of the symbols, secular or profane as they may be, and enable them to be called forth by the symbols to express their faith through action. The key is in how we use the symbols and weave them into the totality of the ritual to accomplish that.

The symbols and actions used in ritual must be broken open to reveal the sacred within them in the same way that we break open the Word and break the Bread in the Eucharist. Very ordinary things—rocks, newspapers, sticks, etc. can be used in ritual and the holiness of them can be revealed through ritual. It is a matter of recognizing the sacred in the symbol as it becomes a part of the total ritual.

The third question concerns itself with the space used for ritual.

Is the space flexible enough to be constituted sacred by the actions and belief of the participants in a ritual or does it dominate and allow only limited "sacred" action?

Any space can be used for ritual. It does not always have to be a designated sacred space such as the church or chapel. In fact, it is usually better if the space is not a church. People and events make a space sacred. Furthermore, the space used for ritual often needs to be more flexible than that of most of our churches and chapels. The ranks of pews and narrow aisles limit the range of action that can take place in a church.

I often use more than one room in ritual, particularly if the ritual calls for a movement symbol or action. I also am careful that I have

It is in freedom that the greatest revelation takes place. Yet, paradoxically freedom involves creative use of discipline.

a large enough room to accomplish what the ritual might call forth in the participants. Using a large empty room enables you to design an environment within that room that is specific for that particular ritual.

The fourth question proposed by Jones is:

Does the ritual structure provide a release and focus of individual and communal energies?

A delicate balance must be maintained between freedom and control in ritual. Without the control that provides direction for individual energies to flow together in ritual, we risk bedlam. And yet our arrangement of time, actions and space needs to allow participants to be free to experience and express their own feelings, beliefs, and even actions.

It is in freedom that the greatest revelation takes place. Yet paradoxically freedom interfaces with creative use of discipline.

If we believe that ritual enables us to express what is in the heart, then in our design of ritual events, we must take care to provide for that expression by individuals within our communities. No matter how deliberately we may design a ritual we must avoid trying to predetermine what will happen and how; we must always be open to the unplanned, to the surprise, and allow for the free use of time and space for that to happen.

Particularly helpful to me in the creation of rituals are the seeds planted by others' rituals and non-ritual experiences. Ideas are shared with me through books, casual conversation, and my own participation in ritual experiences. The sharings of parents during the adults' workshops provide helpful information and ideas as well. Once I decide what it is that we will celebrate in a particular ritual, I begin remembering my own experiences of that event. I also begin remembering what other people have told me about the experiences that they had with it. I recall the stories, songs, poems, scriptures, symbols, which speak to the theme. All of these components provide germs of ideas for ritual.

In a later section of this book, I include some of the rituals which I have used successfully in our family program. Please do not try to use these without modifying them for your purposes. Remember, they were used in a particular place with a particular group of people and usually flowed from some prior considerations of a topic or "teachable moment" with parents. In addition, they were led by a particular person, myself, with a personality different from your own. Creating a ritual demands that the ritual not only be in keeping with the experiences and character of the participants, but that the leader feel totally comfortable with the entire ritual, or it is sure to fail. You may not feel comfortable with any of these rituals. In that case, use those aspects of them that spark ideas and possibilities for your own rituals.

Many families have their own rituals and family experiences that are much more valuable to them than the ones which you or I suggest. Encourage them to continue and also to share their ideas with other families. I have found those times of families sharing with families how they celebrate life are by far the most useful and enspiriting moments of catechesis.

Promote family fun days—one day in each month which the family sets aside and plans to do something special together. Family fun days can be as beneficial as specific family religious activities. I think it is important to help families realize this. Going to a film, a play, a museum, or just staying home around the fireplace with popcorn are as holy a time for families to share as going to church. Sometimes I think we do families a disservice by inundating them with religious activities rather than helping them to see the relationship between faith and life.

Another bit of advice is that in preparing the printed sheet for home rituals, embellish the sheet with attractive art and carefully space the typing to insure greater readability. Nothing is more discouraging to parents than getting an 8 ½ x 11 inch sheet of paper filled with typing. Most people will not even read such a page. The most readily used suggestions are those which are brief and appealing to the eye. Better to use two sheets that will be read and used than one sheet that will be laid aside unread because unappealing in format.

Finally, only use the home ritual idea if your families indicate a desire for such experiences at home. If the need for home activities did not surface in your needs assessment, then don't waste your time providing an unasked for commodity.

Most families, however, do want some sort of suggestions for sharing faith at home with their families and appreciate when you provide them.

At the risk of repeating myself, the best rituals for family use will be simple, natural, fun, and include time for sharing a food treat afterwards. Nothing attracts children like food treats, and ending an activity in that way builds anticipation to have similar activity again. Besides, it is often over the food when everyone is relaxed that the best sharing takes place after the structured activity.

As families become gradually more comfortable with teachable moments and planned rituals, as they experience success with them, their children also begin to place more trust in their parents' ability to share faith. Not long ago at a Sunday liturgy, a four-year-old, whose parents were members of PFL for about three years decided she wanted to sit with me rather than with her parents. To help keep her occupied, she had brought with her a copy of a small illustrated children's bible. In the course of the liturgy, she asked who was in a particular picture. Very matter-of-factly I answered, "Moses." After communion, she returned to her parents for a few minutes. When she came back, she informed me that I was right about the picture. She had asked her mother, and her mother also said it was Moses. Whatever happened to "Sister said. . . ."?

Chapter 7

The Future of Family Catechesis

The Need for a Catechetical Conversion

The Department of Education of the United States Catholic Conference determined in 1978 that only 750 parishes in the country had family programs of some sort. Most of these were sacramental preparation programs. As we strive to implement the Decade of the Family, more and more parishes will be developing family catechetical programs. In most of these parishes, the family program will be considered an alternate model of catechetics. This is unfortunate.

Tradition, as we understand it in the Church, is the handing on of the faith from generation to generation. Psychologists, sociologists, anthropologists and educators have indicated that our basic attitudes, beliefs and faith are determined for the most part by our parents and families. If we really believe this, then we cannot at the same time believe that family catechesis is an alternate model of catechetics.

Family catechesis is the primary catechetical method. It always has been; and unless our society and culture change drastically, it will continue to be. The challenge before us is: how do we capitalize on that foundational element of our culture? How do we alter our attitude to be able to see the other aspects of catechetical programming as auxiliary models which support and assist the fundamental and essential catechetical method—family catechesis?

The family is the basic unit of society and the basic transmitter of faith. Therefore, families deserve our primary catechetical efforts, while CCD classes, children's liturgies, youth programs, learning center activities for children, summer bible schools, church vacation schools, etc. are the handmaids and supporters of family catechesis. The future of family catechesis lies in our viewing family as pivotal for all of our religious education.

Obviously, this requires a massive change of attitude—what I call our "catechetical conversion." Unless it takes place, family catechesis will become something we tried once, and future generations of students will read about it in histories. A conversion of this magnitude will not be easy, but it seems to me it is one with which we must seriously grapple.

This conversion is already happening. As young families are involved in good family programs, they do begin to see the other catechetical offerings we provide as alternatives, while their family experiences remain essential for them. As these families grow older, they are requesting similar catechetical approaches for themselves as families with adolescent children. Parents realize that their young people have to begin to test their autonomy and be introduced to some solid theological knowledge at that age; but at the same time, they want to have some input and participation in that process. As one married couple said to me recently: "We want to know what kind of theology our children will be learning, so that we can continue to learn with them and to share our faith and knowledge as a family—not to coerce them into believing what we do but to help them make the important life decisions that they begin to make at that age."

As we move toward a family approach in parishes, we will have to expand our notion of family, so that every parish member is integrated into the parish family.

Statements of that type have helped us to design an outgrowth of Project Family Life for families with adolescents. Presently it follows a learning model which involves parents and their teen-aged children together, with opportunities built in for the young people to use their own parents in a mentor capacity or to be able to use other adults in that capacity, to help them integrate the information learned. This aspect of the program will be open only to families who have been in the earlier family program for two or more years. Small children will not be a part of this element of the program; it is for teenaged children and their parents only. The program will incorporate ritual into its format but at the same time will involve an introduction to theological content. The same model probably would not be effective for families who have not experienced family catechesis previously. For those who have, however, the concept and approach is needed and requested. The young people may certainly be involved in any of the alternative youth programs and experiences we offer, but the family paradigm will be the basic catechetical program for them.

Other approaches will have to be designed for families who have not been involved in family catechesis. Modifications of a model of this type, which are perhaps less regular or intense, have definite possibilities. Numerous opportunities are open to the parish and director who are convinced of the value of family/youth experiences and catechetics.

I believe that most teenagers are not as eager to alienate themselves from their families as people may think. In a sense, we have convinced ourselves that the teen-parent alienation is inevitable, and it has become a self-fulfilling prophecy. Given opportunities to spend some quality time together without the little ones, and with other similar families, parents and teenagers might surprise us and themselves with their mutual satisfaction and enjoyment with one another.

Whatever our approach either to families with young children or families with teenagers, our parishes must ready themselves to become family focused, with a broadened definition of family. As we move toward a family approach in parishes, we will have to expand our notion of family, so that every parish member sees him/herself integrated into the *parish* family. Basically, what that means is that our parishes need to become family focused and adult-centered communities whose primary role is to share faith with one another.

We will also have to expand our notion of the ways faith is shared and transmitted. The Catholic Church tends to focus the majority of its time, energy and money on educational institutions and programs. (Just check any parish financial report for verification.) Our focussing on family will enable us to see education (narrowly interpreted as doctrinal content or a body of knowledge) as only one dimension of catechesis. As we move through the Decade of the Family, responding with family catechetical programs, we are concurrently moving toward total parish ministry and fuller expressions of our identity as the People of God.

I indicated earlier that a family program can provide one of the best means of integrating the parish ministries of community building, prayer and worship, social action, pastoral care, and education. Family programs are almost always community developers, and the people in the program who have experienced a community spirit on a smaller scale naturally help spread and develop that spirit in the larger community. Families who are enabled to ritualize with one another bring that ability to enact the faith to the larger community and enhance the worship life of others.

Families are much more able to involve themselves in social justice as a family when they can support one another in their efforts. Certainly, a family participating in a social action project is more effective than a fourth or fifth grader or class trying to be socially aware. In the first place, children by themselves have little if any advantageous effect in that area. How much can they be involved in a manner which is truly valuable for either themselves or those they attempt to serve? But with the example and actions of their parents and families in conjunction with other families, the service ministry becomes more authentic and ministerial, and not just a class activity for a week. Within the family context justice and mercy become a way of life.

All of those aspects of parish ministry, coupled with theological learning at appropriate times make for a well-rounded Christian family and Christian community. The various rituals and activities mentioned in the preceding chapters are indications of how this happens, slowly but surely.

The future of family catechesis, then, is supportive of the future of the parish community and *vice versa.* The family will not be able to grow in any of these areas if there is not parish awareness and involvement in these same areas.

Finally, there is nothing like a good family catechetical program to help a parish become aware of the many other aspects of family which require ministry. Someone once said, "You can't preach the Gospel to a hungry person." The same might be said of a hurting family, an alienated teenager, a recently divorced person, a struggling single parent, an aged or ill person, or any of the other categories of people described in the American Bishop's *Pastoral Plan for Family Ministry.*

While I suspect that most parishes will begin implementation of the *Pastoral Plan* through catechetical programs because of our emphasis on education, family ministry cannot stop with family-centered catechetical programs. True, understanding catechesis as broader than religious education is already an extension of family ministry, but there is an even broader emphasis which challenges us.

Religious education was *not* among the top eight general areas in which people wanted more help from their Church according to the 1976 *Call To Action* consultation. Dolores Curran, who served on the Writing Committees for Family for both the Call To Action proceedings and for the Bishop's *Plan of Pastoral Action for Family Ministry,* has pointed out:

. . . people told us that they have prior

Basically that means that our parishes need to become family-focused and adult-centered communities whose primary role is to share faith with one another.

The family is the basic unit of society and the basic transmitter of faith. Therefore, families deserve our primary catechetical efforts. CCD classes, children's liturgies, youth programs, learning center activities for children, summer bible schools, church vacation schools, etc. are the handmaids and supporters of family catechesis.

needs in their family, needs like communicating with one another, handling sensitively the elders in their lives, helping children learn a realistic while moral view of sexuality, dealing with television, and the myriad of problems connected with divorce. . . . Until our families stop hurting in other areas, religious education isn't going to be particularly helpful. If Mom and Dad haven't smiled at each other in a couple of months, it doesn't do much good to set up an elaborate adult education program for them in the parish.

Family ministry hangs in that delicate balance between providing good catechetics for families and at the same time dealing with those pastoral needs of families which can keep them from being enriched by catechesis. Family catechesis can serve as a beginning, based on our educational tradition in the Church. But you will not have a family-cen-

tered program long before you find it necessary to respond to the pastoral needs expressed in the Call To Action Plan: *To Do The Work of Justice: A Plan of Action For the Catholic Community in the United States* (NCCB, May 4, 1978) and the *Plan of Pastoral Action for Family Ministry* (NCCB, May 4, 1978). In each of these, our bishops, speaking for our Catholic people, have held out a powerful challenge to us.

Every parish is going to have to take a serious look at itself and at the way in which it ministers totally to family. Parishes may have to completely re-evaluate their goals and objectives. They may have to realign or hire more staff. They may have to provide less elaborate programs of religious education and more elaborate programs of pastoral care, faith sharing, community building, one-to-one ministry, and family growth and enrichment (which is not synonymous with family-centered religious education). They may have to encourage their Diocesan Family Life Commissions, Religious Education Departments, Liturgy and Catholic Charities Departments to work more closely together in order to better serve both the individual parishes and the diocese in terms of ministry to families. They may have to, as some suggest, *suspend* all religious education in the parish and spend a year re-assessing needs and goals. They may have to be prepared to eliminate some staff in order to hire trained and experienced family ministers. They may have to provide extensive inservice training for present staff before attempting family ministry. Or, the parish may be ready to launch into a family approach to catechesis and ministry because of an already existing parish vision and preparation.

What is important to remember in designing and developing family programs is that it is possible to include all areas of parish ministry in a catechetical program. That is the value of seeing the program as precisely catechetical rather than as strictly educational. But even at that, it is still only a prelude to your parish's total approach to family ministry. In time, as the implementation of family ministry develops, the totality of the community's ministerial action will be able to be seen as family focused and adult centered against the backdrop of a broad vision of the implementation of the renewed *Rite of Christian Initiation for Adults,* which I think has incredible implications for total parish renewal.

Is there hope that we can do so much? I

the faith of the family than in the religious instruction of the children. We have a timetable and a challenge to meet the needs of the family holistically and catechetically in the decade of the 80's.

There is hope that we can do so, but not assurance. Our success will depend on our own faith, not only in the Trinity, but in the

---

We have to expand our notion of the ways faith is shared and transmitted. The Catholic Church in the U.S. tends to focus the majority of its time, energy and money on educational institutions and programs.

---

definitely believe so. Again I quote Dolores Curran from her *Family: A Catechetical Challenge for the 80's* (a Resource Paper for the National Conference of Diocesan Directors of Religious Education):

I am more hopeful now than I was ten years ago when I was idealistic and unrealistic in expecting parishes to meet needs that they hadn't yet perceived. Those family needs are now articulated and obvious. Our bishops have not only validated the idea of family ministry but have authorized a vision and a strategy. . . .

Ministry to the family will take time to sift down from the bishops, the USCC, papers like this one, and the many excellent family workshops now being offered our parish leadership. More pastors are becoming educated to family ministry. Among professional religious educators, the concept of family catechesis is being broadened to include the total family environment within the total parish family structure. We are utilizing authorities and studies on the family from many disciplines—psychology, sociology, education—to flesh out our theology. We are becoming more interested in

sureness of our vision and in our perseverance in working toward achievement of this oldest but newest form of ministry—the family.

Our challenge is to launch out creatively in the area of family. Develop programs for your people which are in keeping with their expressed needs, ritualize and share faith with them. But don't do any of that without a view of the total ministerial panorama and in cooperation with the other areas of ministry in your parish community. Without that integration, you will be merely proliferating yet another religious educational experiment which will slowly die for want of wholeness. I am optimistic that we can do it, but I think we must roll up our sleeves for more than a year, perhaps for even more than a decade.

We can do it with creativity, awareness of the needs of people, nourishment from other ministerial areas and reciprocal nourishment to those areas, patience, perseverance, determination, and a commitment to the Christian family in its broadest definition. If any institution can serve the total needs of the family, the Church can. Because the Church is, after all, the total Christian community.

Chapter 8

Family Rituals

For Parish and Neighborhood Settings

In this section of the book, I have gathered examples of family activities and rituals which I celebrated with families of PFL. The first eight rituals were designed and used at our family workshops in the parish setting. The next six rituals were designed and used by small groups of families in their neighborhood settings. The last one is an example of what one family did for their baby's baptism.

In Chapter 9, I have gathered many ideas for helping families to understand and celebrate seasonal/liturgical events in their homes.

I hope and intend that the materials in both these chapters will inspire you to design your own. Do not attempt to use the rituals as they are presented herein. Adapt them for use with your people and in your circumstances. Rituals should be a personal expression of the faith of the community celebrating. Otherwise they become mechanical and removed from the experience of that community.

Finally, I am including a bibliography of materials that I have referred to at different times in this book and resources that I have found helpful in my own understanding and implementing of family catechesis and ritualizing.

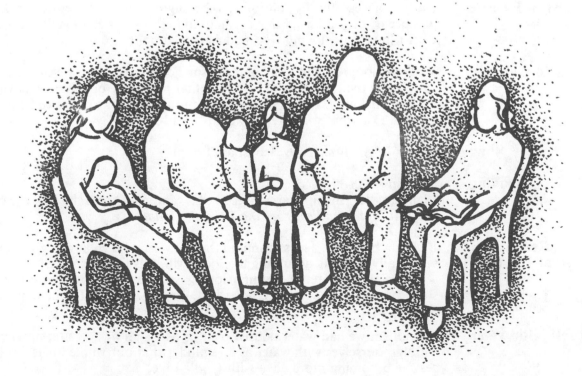

A Ritual of Belonging and Renewal of Baptism

Pre-ritual activity	Separate those with blue and brown eyes. Spend about three to four minutes talking to only one group and disregarding the other group. Then bring the groups together.
Discuss	How do you feel when you don't belong? How did you feel about not being able to include the other people? Have you ever been rejected? Have you ever rejected someone before tonight? What should we as Christians do if someone is left out? Who in this room has been baptized? What happened to us in baptism?
Film	*Baptism* (TeleKETICS production by Franciscan Communications Center)
Family sharing	(Discussion guide included with film)
Ritual action	All with arms outstretched to one another: We the Christian Community welcome you with great joy. We claim you for Christ by the Sign of the Cross. (All families sign one another on the forehead with the Christian sign of the cross.)
Questions to Parents	Do you accept the responsibility of bringing up your children in the practice of the faith, to bring them up to keep God's commandments as Christ taught us, loving God and our neighbor?
Questions to Children	Will you look first to your parents for good example, listen to them, and follow their example of love for other people? Good! We all have a big responsibility. Let us now pray the prayer of St. Francis to help us be aware of what we have answered "yes" to:
Song	*Prayer of St. Francis* by Sebastian Temple
Reading	*Matthew* 3:13-17 Light candles. In baptism, we received a candle, lit from the Easter candle. *(All light candles from the Paschal Candle.)*
Renewal of Baptismal Promises	By being baptized, Jesus promised that he would be willing to give himself totally to living according to God's will. His life became Eucharist: a thanksgiving offered through loving service. In baptism we made some promises too. Let's renew those promises now: (from Baptism Rite)
Blessing self with water	In baptism we had water poured over us as a sign of new life; now, we will sign ourselves with water as a reminder that our whole life is a process of becoming more alive with God's love.

Prayer   *Parents:* Lord, God, we are happy to be called your people, and to hand on to our children the gift of life and the touch of love. We thank you for all your gifts to us: for our parents, these our friends, this your Church, and for our home and our children, the flowers of our love. We will listen for your Spirit in all of these. Through your Spirit we open our hearts to the needs that you have made flesh in our children and to the needs of everyone we meet, for it is from the warmth of our bodies and the gentleness of our hands that our children will come to learn how gentle is your love. Amen.

Children: God, we are happy to be called your children. We thank you for our parents, our friends, our Church and our homes. Help us to listen to our parents and follow their good example, so that the light of your love will shine through us to others.

All: Lord God, you call us in your Spirit to be an example to one another. May we be ready to give true Christian love to warm one another. Send us the light of your Spirit, as you always do, so that we will be able to see others' needs, that from the gifts You have given each of us, we may share with others. This we ask in the name of your own son, Jesus. Amen.

Final blessing   God, the Creator, is the giver of all life. Through Jesus, God has brought joy to all Christian parents. May God bless all parents here. You are the first teachers of your children in the ways of faith. May you also be the best of teachers, bearing witness to the faith by what you do and say. Jesus revealed God's love for children, and asked that they be brought close to him. May God bless all children here. You are a joy to your parents. May you always be so by the way that you live and act toward one another. And may God bless us all in the sign of the life-giving Cross and in the name of the Father, and of the Son, and of the Holy Spirit. All: Amen.

Closing song   *I've Got A Light* by Sr. Roberta McGrath, R.S.M.

——————Family Ritual of Reconciliation

Materials   Two small stones for each person
Film: *Names of Sin* from TeleKETICS by Franciscan Communication Center
Three or four metal pails

Film   *Names of Sin*

Family sharing   Good discussion questions are provided with the film. After allowing about 10 or 15 minutes for discussion, all move to another room singing: *O Healing River* (Baptist folk hymn). As families enter the room, they are instructed to take two stones from the containers and to hold them tightly in their hands.

Dialogue   Leader talks with the group about how the stones feel, how they are getting warm and more comfortable in their hands, how with a little imagination, they could become pets. Relate that to our "pet sins," our "pet nasties." Discuss how hard it is to hug someone or shake hands with a stone held tightly in our hands, how all that is thought about is the stone being held.

Naming sins   What are the names of those stones we hold? One of them might be *Simon Sasser,* (describe the actions that accompany each name, e.g., he talks back when he's asked to do something; he makes what he thinks are smart remarks to people; he usually does these things to adults and his tone of voice is usually unkind. Others might be:
    Louie Liar
    Polly Poke-Fun
    Nancy Non-Pray-er
    Gloria Gossip
    Oscar Overworker
    Charlie Cheater and Suzy Stealer (twins)
    Nellie Non-Listener
    Andy Anger
    Billy Bully
    Thomas Too-Busy
After the leader has suggested some names and descriptions for the stones (sins), participants are asked to name the stones that they are holding along with descriptions. (If the leader's naming is done dramatically and slightly humorously, participants feel free to join in readily using a similar tone.) After the naming, allow a short time for reflection.

Scripture   *Ezekiel 36:25-28*

Ritual action   Get rid of the stones.
Names of sin are called off by the leader. As the name that participants have given their stones is announced, they rise and toss their stones into the metal pails provided at various places among the group. As the stones sound in the pails, the group calls out "Let it go!" and applaud the participants who have released their stones. When participants have rid themselves of both stones, they may pick up a "Peace Sign" (a decorated piece of paper with the word *peace* written on it).

Final prayer   Hold hands and pray or sing the Lord's Prayer.

Sing   *Shalom Chaverim* (traditional Jewish round) or form a circle dance and sing: *Lord of the Dance* by Sidney Carter.

———— A Thank-God-For-Parents Ritual

Opening prayer   *Leader*

Scripture   *Proverbs* 31:10, 12, 20, 25, 28, 29 (paraphrased and read as a choral reading by two groups of children)

Side A	*Side B*
1) The perfect Mom is worth more than the price of pearl	1) The perfect Dad is worth more than the price of gold
2) Help and not hurt, she brings all the days of her life.	2) Help and not hurt he brings all the days of his life
3) She holds out her hand to the poor	3) He holds out his hand to the poor.
4) She opens her arms to the needy	4) He opens his arms to the needy
5) She is clothed in strength and dignity	5) He is clothed in strength and dignity.
6) She can laugh at the days to come	6) He can laugh at the days to come
7) Her children stand and praise her; so does her husband	7) His children stand and praise him; so does his wife

8) *Both sides together,* loudly: There are many fine parents in the world,
   but you are the best of them all.

Activity   On papers provided, please write to your children/parents something positive that you have always wanted to tell them, but haven't lately. I suggest that those too young to write can draw a special picture for their parents. When everyone is finished, exchange the papers. Children give theirs to their parents; parents give theirs to their children.

Song   *Thank You, Lord* by Carey Landry
Thank you Lord, for giving us Moms. *(Children only)*
Thank you Lord, for giving us Dads. *(Children only)*
Thank you Lord, for giving us children. *(Parents only)*
Thank you Lord, for giving us us. *(Everyone)*

Scripture   *Ephesians* 6:1-5

Ritual action   Take some time now to show one another through some non-verbal sign, how you feel about one another.

Song   *Joy, Joy, Joy* (traditional)
The ritual then moved into another room that the children had decorated for a party for their parents. Children did all of the serving. The entire evening was a total surprise for parents which left not a few of them misty-eyed.

A Fuzzy Tale

Needed   colored yarn and scissors

Story   *A Fuzzy Tale* by Claude Steiner. Tell the story using props: a warm fuzzy (a yarn pom pom); a cold prickly (a styrofoam ball with colored toothpicks stuck into it); a warm fuzzy with string attached (a yarn pom pom with a longer piece of yarn attached to it). (This story is also in film form from Mass Media Ministries, 2116 N. Charles St., Baltimore, MD 21218.)

Family sharing   When do your parents, . . . children . . . sisters . . . brothers . . . give you warm fuzzies . . . cold pricklies . . . warm fuzzies with strings attached . . . ?

Make a family fuzzy   Using the yarn provided, each family makes a large family fuzzy. This fuzzy is to be passed around the family during the week so that each person has it for a time and has the love and care that goes with it.

Song   Choose an appropriate song.

Litany   *Leader:* We are here and we can smile
All: We can reach out to each other and share the warmth of loving
Leader: There will be exciting times—
All: When love is given and received and given back again. The love will be alive and we can watch it grow and become.
Leader: There may be scary times—
All: When it seems our reaching out is rejected and it may make us feel strange and hurt
Leader: But love is strong and can survive those scary times.
All: And love is warm and can surround us with a safe place where we are each accepted.
Leader: And love is contagious. We will be able to watch it spread from person to person.
All: And love multiplies and becomes more, and never ever runs out.

Song   *Magic Penny* by Melvina Reynolds

Ritual Action   Give a FUZZIES cheer using family fuzzies like pom poms and having the individual letters of the word on pieces of tagboard to be spelled out.

Scripture   1 Corinthians 13: 4-8

Prayer   (Asking for love and the ability to return love)

Song   *Magic Penny* repeated while all form a circle with arms around one another. At the conclusion of the song, give one another a warm fuzzy stroke.

I. The Gathering of the Gifted

Materials   Gift wrapping paper, ribbon, tape, scissors, pencils, crayons, colored paper on which to write.
Each family is asked to bring a small box with them to the ritual.

Introduction   Conversation about God-given gifts

Family sharing   a) With families sitting in circles with backs to each other, each person writes or draws what s/he considers to be his/her personal gifts.

b) That completed, families face each other and tell what their gifts are.

c) Families then share with each member the gifts that they see in that family member.

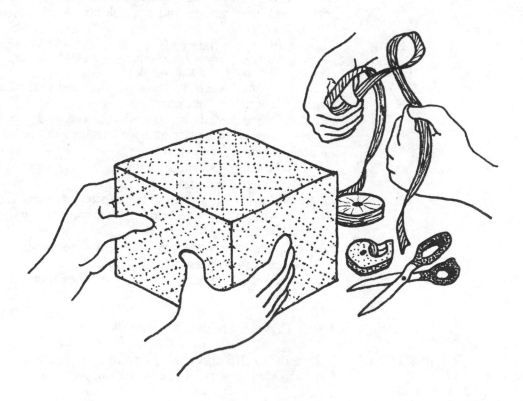

II. We Are Gifts

God has given each of us gifts, and we are gifts to God. Can you think of things you like about each person in the family that God would like, too?

Have one person at a time sit in the middle of the family circle as all the others tell what each likes about him or her. Have a "family secretary" record the information.

What My Family Likes About Me

Name _____

Comments _____

_____

_____

d) Each family puts individual gift papers and family gift paper into the box they brought, wraps the box with gift wrapping and ribbon, and puts the family name on it.

Procession

Move to another room holding gifts high singing:
We are gifted, We are gifted
Yes, we are, Yes, we are.
People very gifted, People very gifted
Yes, that's us, Yes, that's us.

We are special, We are special
Yes, we are, Yes, we are.
Someone very special, Someone very special
Yes, that's us, Yes, that's us.
(Melody: *Are You Sleeping, Brother John*)

Group sharing

Have families call out some of the gifts that were mentioned in their family sharing. After each family's statement, the group responds, "The gift you have received, give as a gift," and applauds.

Scripture

I Corinthians 12:1, 4-7 (paraphrased)

Song or music

Choose an appropriate song that all can sing or a musical selection (such as "All Good Gifts" from *Godspel*) that can be played while the families do the ritual action which follows:

Ritual action

Each family places gifts around a large plant or a leafless tree to remain there until the next meeting.

Closing prayer

Final prayer of praise and blessing by the leader.

_____ III. Commissioned as Ministers

Pre-ritual preparation   Prior to the ritual rehearse the play, *The Case of the Innocent Stomach*, which is printed following this ritual. Be sure to have actors of all ages. Make props which include tagboard cutouts of each of the body parts in the play for actors to carry on or wear on strings around their necks.

Welcome and greeting   *Leader*

Scripture   *1 Corinthians* 12:12-27

Play   *The Case of the Innocent Stomach* (origin unknown)

Family sharing   What is the play trying to say to us?
What can we learn from this play?
What does it say about ministry and being a minister?

Song   *They'll Know We Are Christians* by Peter Scholtes

Prayer   *Leader:* Blessing of oil and prayer of commissioning to go out and use our gifts to minister to others.

Anointing   Leader anoints parents. Parents return to their families and anoint each family member with the words: "You are a special gift, go now and use it for others."

Song   *Priestly People* by Lucien Deiss

Return gifts   *Leader:* We have been anointed to go out and use the gifts in these boxes to minister to others. Take them and use them to the best of your ability. (Families come up to reclaim their "Gift Boxes")

Prayer   (of thanksgiving)

Song   *Witness Song* by Robert Blue

The Play: The Case of the Innocent Stomach

Scene I: HEAD enters from one side of the playing area; EYES and EARS from the other.
HEAD: Hello, EYES, have you seen anything interesting lately?
EYES: We don't miss a thing. And we don't like what we see.
HEAD: Is that so? Well, EARS, what have you heard?
EARS: We hear plenty. All the members are complaining. (MOUTH, NOSE and BODY enter.)

HEAD: I'm sorry to hear that. What seems to be the trouble?

MOUTH: It's STOMACH. All the rest of us members of the body work hard to feed STOMACH.

NOSE: All stomach ever does is take what we give him. He never gives us anything.

BODY: He's so lazy and greedy. We're all angry at him. (ARMS, LEGS, HANDS and FEET enter.)

HANDS: We've all been talking about this. I think something should be done.

HEAD: Let me get this straight. All you members of the body feel that you work hard gathering food just so STOMACH can enjoy himself. And STOMACH gives you nothing in return.

ALL: (angrily) Yes!

HEAD: Well, what do you think should be done?

LEGS: We'll just stop working. I won't walk to the store to get food.

EYES: I won't look around for food.

ARMS: I won't get any food to MOUTH.

MOUTH: And I won't chew any food.

FEET: We'll teach STOMACH a lesson. He'll be sorry. Everyone has to do his or her share.

HEAD: All right. We'll try it and see what happens.

Scene II: Sign carrier crosses the front of the playing area carrying the sign: TWO DAYS LATER. All actors in the playing area except HEAD sit or half-lie down, looking weak and dejected.

ARMS: Oh, I'm so tired, I'm not strong anymore.

EYES: I agree. I'm so weak. Everything is getting blurry.

EARS: (loudly) I can't hear you. Speak a little louder. What's that ringing sound I hear?

MOUTH: I'm getting stiff from not working.

NOSE: It's been so long since I smelled good food.

LEGS: I can't even stand up. I don't understand. STOMACH is the one who's supposed to be suffering, not us. What can we do?

ARMS: Maybe we were wrong about STOMACH. Do you suppose he really was working all the time, but we didn't know it?

FEET: He must have been quietly doing his job and supplying us with strength and nourishment. All the time we thought he was selfish and lazy.

BODY: We haven't been fair to STOMACH.

(STOMACH enters smiling, and crosses to where HEAD is standing. HEAD embraces STOMACH.)

HEAD: You members of the body have learned a good lesson. Now, let's all get back to our jobs.

All come together, shake hands, and take a bow.

IV. We Are Ministers

Note: The adult workshop preceding this particular ritual included the following at-home activity:

Family Ministry Log

Pre-ritual preparation

The Family Ministry Log is an instrument to help the family and individuals in the family to recognize the many ways in which they minister to one another and to other families and individuals. It can also help to improve a family's desire to serve others better and to live out the exhortation we all have to be ministers of the Word.

1. Sometime this week, sit down with the family and your spiral notebook.
2. Talk about ways that individual family members minister to (serve-help) one another and the total family. (A review of the Family Workshop discussion on gifts might be helpful.)
   Discuss: a) What gifts that each family member has, helped that person minister to or serve/help the family?
   b) In what other ways do individual family members minister to the family and to individual family members?
   c) How has our whole family ministered to other individuals and families?
   d) How have individuals ministered to others outside the family?
   e) How might each of us minister even better to our family? Let each person answer for her/himself.
   f) How might our family minister even better to others?
3. Explain that the notebook is going to be a *Family Ministry Log* in which each person writes or draws the ways that they ministered to others each day.
4. Divide the notebook into as many sections as there are family members with one section for the total family.
5. Mark the sections with tabs and write family members' names on the tabs, e.g., "Mom," "Dad," "Trish," "Oscar," and "Family."
6. Explain how each person will record their ministerial (helping) activities in the notebook beginning with today.
   e.g., "Tuesday, January 15—Shoveled neighbor's walk, refused pay."
   Once each week—or more often, if you'd like—sit down as a family. Talk about ways in which the whole family ministered to others and record it in the Log.
   e.g., "Sunday, January 22—Gave ride to family whose car wasn't working."
7. End the evening with spontaneous prayer for help in your family's desire to minister better—don't forget prayers of thanks and praise

for the many gifts that have been given to each family member and to your total family together. Then have a treat—(play a game together, have hot cocoa or popcorn, etc.)

Bring your notebook to the January Family Workshop

Ritual

Story	Film *Follow Me* by Family Films
Family sharing	Get together with another family, someone you don't know very well and share your ideas about the film. (Discussion guide included with the film)
Song and circle dance	*Prayer of St. Francis* by Sebastian Temple. For the dance, the group forms two circles, one inside the other. As the refrain of the song is sung, the circles move in opposite directions with hands extended to touch one another, as a sign of willingness to reach out to others in love and service. (This symbolic action is better not explained.)
Group sharing	Families share with the group some of the ministerial actions they have recorded in their Ministry Logs.
Prayer	(Of praise and thanks)
	Song and Circle Dance repeated.

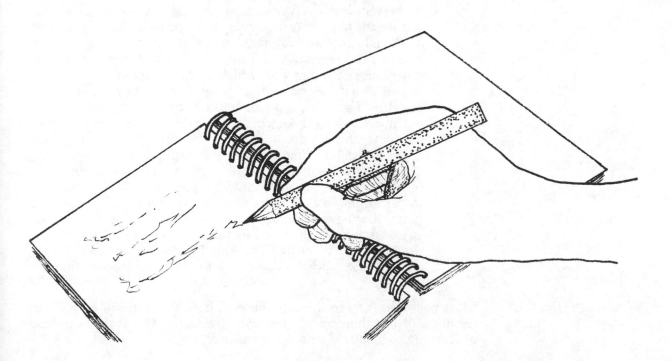

Neighborhood Family Ritual
First Week of Lent

The next five rituals were designed for use in neighborhood groups of four or five families during Lent. They are adapted from The Liturgical Conference's *Ashes to Easter* and *Major Feasts and Seasons*.

Theme	Lent as Struggle
Symbol	Bare branch, twig forming a cross.
Materials	Twigs or branches for making cross Yarn Bible
Introduction **(parents' background)**	Explain Family Prayer Night as a time not for learning or teaching anything but for praying and sharing faith together. Opening prayer may be given by anyone. Scripture read by anyone in the group. Song—part of prayer. Prayer—praise, thanks, petition. Silence—enjoy it, relax with it.
Opening prayer	Let us begin our prayer as we begin all prayer in our tradition with the Sign of the Cross. . . . In the Name of the Father, etc.
Scripture **(parents' background)**	*Matthew 4:1-11* *Leader:* Jesus went into the desert to fast and pray in preparation for his ministry. Every year, as a Church, we summon ourselves to be renewed by fasting and praying and other practices. We see the need to turn around some parts of our life, almost as though to start over again. It's a struggle like the struggle between the tempter and Jesus. Jesus was tempted with the same kinds of things with which we are tempted: to be preoccupied with things rather than people; to do showy things such as get a bigger car, a bigger and better camper, another new outfit, a ten-speed bike when a three- or five-speed is probably adequate; to worship something other than God. What *things* do we worship? (Time given to some spontaneous responses.) The gospel writer makes it look very easy for Jesus, but scripture scholars say he may only be summarizing the struggles with temptation that Jesus faced every day of his public life. Remember he was human like us—and the gospel writer, like any of us who might be really taken up with someone special, would like to paint him as God. Biographers often do that. How can Lent help us *come to grips* with evil the way that Jesus did?
Silent reflection	Close your eyes for a couple of minutes. Think about one or both of the readings, or just think about your own breathing. This is the beginning of learning to meditate—Enjoy the silence.

Faith sharing   What do the scriptures say to you personally? Let's share that belief.

Shared prayer   Mention a strength that is needed in these times—
By ourselves personally
By the Church
By the community
By the world.
Then prayers of praise and thanks for strengths that individuals, families, communities have—or have received.

Activity   We all have hateful things we really have to struggle with. Things we want to take out of our lives. Family members write or express through drawing or paper-tearing the one thing that they are going to struggle with this Lent. Attach them with yarn to cross made of twigs. (Hold cross high)

Song   *Kumbaya* (West Indies Traditional) Someone's struggling . . . , praying . . . , growing . . . , etc.)

Scripture   1 Cor. 9:24-27 (Paul tells about how life is a struggle and a contest).

Blessing of the crosses   *Leader:* These crosses are symbols of our lenten struggle to be like Jesus; let us now bless them together.
One person in the family holds the cross high. Everyone else holds hands, palms up toward the cross, and responds "Bless these crosses, Lord," after each statement:
As a sign of Jesus' death and resurrection . . . Bless . . .
As a sign of our death and resurrection to new life . . . Bless . . .
As a sign of Jesus' struggle with evil . . . Bless . . .
As a sign of our struggle with evil . . . Bless . . .
As a sign of our love of Jesus . . . Bless . . .
As a sign of our love for one another . . . Bless . . .
Leader: Give the cross a place of honor at home so it will be a reminder of all we have prayed about tonight and of our individual struggle during Lent.

Lord's Prayer   Join hands.

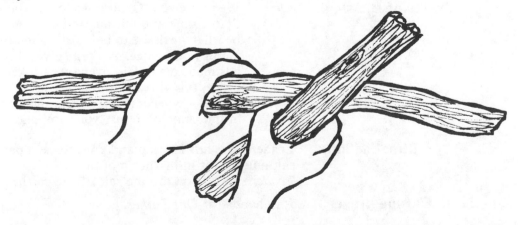

Neighborhood Family Ritual
Second Week of Lent

Theme	God's Call
Symbol	Salt
Materials	Bowl of salt, Bible
Introduction	Real faith is simple and ordinary, so a simple and ordinary symbol like salt is one of the best signs for us people who try to believe—as Abraham did. Salt, too, is "wholemaking;" its flavor spreads through the whole substance to which it is added. We celebrate our call by God then under the symbol of salt—free, simple, and pervasive.
Scripture	*Isaiah* 43:1-4
Silent reflection	
Faith sharing	*Leader:* What do the readings say to you personally? How does/has God called you?
Shared prayer	*Leader:* Let's join in prayer by saying thanks to God for some person whose response to God's call has been a source of personal inspiration and strength, (e.g., Mom, Pope John XXIII, Teresa of Calcutta, a neighbor, etc.).
	Prayers of petition asking for strength to respond to God's call in all the everyday ways that it comes, (e.g., alarm clock, spending more time with children, etc.).
Song	*Kumbaya* ("Someone's praying . . . calling . . . answering . . .")
Closing	*Leader:* One of the ways Jesus talked about our call to live in the world was by saying, "You are the salt of the earth." Complete the statement: "As a Christian, I am like salt because------" What qualities does salt have that we want to have?
Scripture	*Matthew* 5:13 *Mark* 9:50 *Luke* 14:34-35: Readings by three different people. Read one after the other while someone holds up bowl of salt.
Prayer of Blessing	*All:* We praise you, O God; we thank you for your Word. Let your Spirit come upon us all, and over our community that we may be what we desire to be—sisters and brothers to all in works of mercy and justice. We praise you for salt which your Church has made a sign of covenant, a token of friendship, faith and peace, full of zest and flavor. Bless this salt, Lord, and bless us so that we become like salt in the world. We make this prayer in the name of Jesus, your son and our brother. Amen.
Ritual action	Leader takes bowl of salt and goes to each person who takes a pinch of salt and puts it in his/her mouth. *Leader says:* "You are the salt of the earth."
Closing prayer	Join hands for *Our Father*.

Neighborhood Family Ritual
Third Week of Lent

Theme	Thirst for Living Water
Symbol	Water
Materials	Pitcher of icewater, paper cups, paper towel for each person; bible
Opening prayer	(someone in the group)
Scripture	*Psalm* 42:1-2 *John* 4:5-20, 39-42 (Tell the story or assign individuals to read the parts of each character in the story, e.g., woman, Jesus, narrator.)
Silent reflection	
Shared prayer and faith	Prayer of Thanksgiving for water. (This may take the form of briefly telling personal experiences with thirst and end with thanks to God for how the thirst was finally satisfied.) This may lead to discussion of great things water does for us. Prayer of thanks for water as a source of beauty.
Song	*Michael, Row Your Boat Ashore*
Scripture	*Revelations* 22:17
Blessing	*Leader:* We give you thanks, O God, that you come to us in things we can sense. We praise you for your gift of water: Water that touches us with a power beyond our lives, Water that stirs and brings forth living things, Water that cleans stains and grime from all your creatures, Water that sustains grass and plants and trees, Water that refreshes us when we are tired and worn, Water that quenches thirst, Water that surrounds and supports and makes life exciting, Water that soothes and shocks, We praise you with this water. May your Holy Spirit make this water an experience of your love for us, an experience of all that your care for us means—cleansing and refreshing. Then when Easter comes, we may renew our baptism in water.
Ritual action	All drink a glass of water, then dip towels in water and wipe one another's faces to experience the refreshment of water.

Neighborhood Family Ritual
Fourth Week of Lent

Theme	Life and death
Symbol	Seeds
Materials	Container with soil, seeds, (bean, marigold, etc.) and a bible.

Introduction (parents' background)

Easter Sunday is directly tied to the arrival of spring. (Easter is always the first Sunday following the first full moon following the first day of spring.) Passover itself was a spring festival—a way of celebrating the return of life to the earth. For the Jews, it came to mark also a historical event—the Exodus, the coming to the life of freedom from the death of slavery. So this week in our gatherings, we would hope to become more conscious of the wonder of life emerging from death. That prepares us to hear again the passion and death of Jesus, and to celebrate Easter. It prepares us to see that in the ways we "die" in everyday existence, we are being called to rise again. The tiny seed seems the perfect symbol of this. Jesus himself used it: "Unless the grain of wheat falls into the ground and dies, it remains alone. But if it dies, it brings forth much fruit." That mystery is on the level of physical life all that we have to live by. Christian faith has seen in this the meaning of our whole commitment to Jesus: a dying to selfishness, a dying to all the other 'gods' that demand our allegiance in order to live in Christ, to live for other people. We look at a seed and we should see ourselves.

Scriptures

Ezekiel 37:1-14; *John* 11:1-45

Shared prayer

Praise and thanks for any experience of death and resurrection: in nature, in people, in social life, in faith, everywhere; e.g., sorrow and forgiveness after anger and malice toward someone, for joy in one who had been depressed, for health in one who has been sick, for signs of resurrection in nature.

Discuss

Seeds as sign of death and life.

Scripture

John 12:24-25

Ritual action

Plant seeds

Blessing of mini-gardens

All: Bless these seeds, Lord, strengthen them in the gentle movement of soft winds and warm sun; refresh them with rain, and let them grow to full maturity for the good of all.

Final prayer with actions

by Jack Miffleton
(Begin in squatting position) God our Father help us grow *(rise to standing position)* to be flowers for your land. Do not let us grow crooked *(bend from waist)* because we didn't listen to what you wanted from us. Do not let us be blown over by the winds of selfishness *(sway)*. But let us grow straight and strong *(stand straight, arms over head)*, reaching up to you and out to our brothers and sisters. Amen.

Neighborhood Family Ritual
Fifth Week of Lent

Theme	Strength through the Word and the Community
Symbol	Hands
Materials	Bible

Opening prayer   *Leader:* Someone once said: ''The Church's hands are not always clean, but soiled hands are better than no hands at all.'' We are the Church's hands, even though we are soiled. We're not quite perfect; we have been commissioned to provide strength through those hands—strength we get through God's Word, through the Church's sacraments, through one another.

First reading   *Col.* 3:9-14 (We are new people now—we have a general rule of Christian behavior)

Second reading   *Matt.* 8 & 9 (*Matt.* 8:1-2, 8:14-15, 9:23-26) The importance of the touch of Jesus and of our touch. (These stories could be told instead of read.) Silent reflection and discussion of readings.

Shared prayer   *Leader:* Let us pray tonight for the strength to reach out with the Word and with our hands to touch others as Jesus did.
Let us also thank God for people who have touched our lives in a special way. Let us also thank God for God's word and for the ways that it touches us specially.

Song   *Kumbaya* (someone's praying . . . touching . . . loving. . . .)

Reading   *2 Tim.* 4:1-2, 5 (We are charged to preach the Word, Good News)

Ritual action   *Leader holds a bible before each member of the group and says:* ''Will you accept the Word, preach it in your speaking and acting, and reach out to touch others with the kindness and gentleness of Jesus?

(Each member responds and kisses the bible.)

People stand in groups of two, facing each other. They place their hands on each other's shoulders firmly in a gesture of forgiveness, reconciliation and invocation of the Holy Spirit. Keep them there for a few moments. Then offer one another a hug of peace.

A Pre-Easter Ritual

Pre-ritual preparation
Prior to this ritual families were asked to make or purchase a 3" x 9" or 12" white or yellow candle to bring with them to the ritual.

Materials
Enough acrylic paints and brushes for the group.
Film: *Phos* from TeleKETICS by Franciscan Communications Center

View film
Phos

Silent reflection
Room remains totally dark except for one candle burning

Prayer
Leader

Scripture
Matthew 5:14-16

Song
What You Hear In The Dark by Dan Schutte, S.J.

Trust walk
All parents are blindfolded. Children lead them, following a leader who carries the candle, to another room in which many candles are lit and arranged throughout the room.

Scripture
John 3:19-21
Children are then instructed to remove their parents' blindfolds. Allow time for the effect of the room and the preceding Scripture to speak to participants.

Song
Those Who See Light (unknown)

Activity
In an adjoining room, acrylic paints are available for families to decorate their own Easter candles.

Blessing
When all are finished, each family holds their candle high while other members of the family extend hands toward the candle and pray a prayer of blessing for the candles:

Lord, our God, Creator of light, we ask your blessing on this symbol of Christ, our Light. May it be a constant reminder to all of us that we, too, are to bring the Light of Christ to others. Amen.

It is then suggested that the families bring their candles to the Easter Vigil to light from the Paschal Candle. They might also carry the Easter Light home with them as is customary in the Greek Orthodox tradition and which is depicted in the film.

Megan Jean McLellan's Baptism

Greeting by the celebrant

Welcome into the Christian community and "signing" with the cross

      All: Megan, we the Christian Community welcome you with great joy. We claim you for Christ Our Savior by the sign of his cross.

              (Celebrant, parents and godparents now trace the sign of the cross on Megan's forehead. We invite all families to sign one another and Megan with the same Christian sign.)

Procession and Song to the place of the celebration of God's Word

      I Am The Bread Of Life by Suzanne Toolin

Celebration of God's Word	First Reading: *Romans* 6:3-5 (Mike McClellan) Sung Response: *All:* *My Shepherd Is The Lord* by Joseph Gelineau Gospel: *John* 3:1-6 (Grandpa McClellan) Homily: *Celebrant*
General intercessions	*Celebrant*
Anointing with the oil of catechumens	*Celebrant*
Blessing of water	On a small table in front of the altar platform are several containers of water. Members of the McClellan and Newman families will each bring a container to the baptismal font and pour it into the font as the celebrant blesses the baptismal water.
Renunciation of evil and profession of faith	*Celebrant* *All* respond.
The Baptism	(by immersion)
Sung response	*All:* *The Prayer of St. Francis* by Sebastian Temple (Change the word from "me" to "her" as the song is a prayer of blessing for Megan.
Anointing with Chrism	*Celebrant*
Clothing with white garment	*Ellen Neuman, godmother*
The lighted candle	*Dick Neuman, godfather*
Concluding rite	*Celebrant:* My sisters and brothers, Megan has been born as a child of God. Her baptism so signifies. Her sacramental confirmation at a later

age will signify that she is ready to enter more fully into the life of being Christian. The Eucharist will nourish her and be her act of praise and thanksgiving along with her brother Jesus. Let us now pray in her name, as we have acted in her name, calling upon God, in the words Jesus taught us:

All: The Lord's Prayer

Patty and Mike: God, our Father, we are happy to be called your people, and to hand on to our children the gift of life and the touch of love. We thank you for all your gifts to us: for *our* parents, these our friends, this your Church, for our home, our children, and for Megan, the flower of our love. Send us your Spirit. Through your Spirit, open our hearts to the needs that you have made flesh in Megan and to the needs of everyone we meet; for it is from the warmth of our bodies and the gentleness of our hands, that our daughter Megan will come to learn how gentle is your love. Amen.

All: God, you call us in your Spirit to be an example to your daughter, Megan. May we always be ready to provide true Christian love to warm her life. Send us the light of your Spirit, as you always do, so that we will be able to see her needs; that from the gifts that you have given each of us, she may receive your light and love through us. This we ask in the name of your own son, Jesus, and in the power of your Spirit in him. Amen.

Celebrant: God is the giver of all life. Through Jesus, God has brought joy and comfort to all Christian parents.

May God bless Mike and Patty, and bless all parents here. You are the first teachers of your children in the ways of faith. May you be also the best of teachers, bearing witness to the faith by what you say and do, in Christ Jesus, our Lord.

And may God bless us all in the sign of the life-giving cross and in the name of the Father, and of the Son, and of the Holy Spirit.

All: Amen!

Closing song of rejoicing

They'll Know We Are Christians by Peter Scholtes

Suggestion for the future

Celebrate the baptismal days as well as the birthdays in your families. Bring out the baptismal certificate, the white garment and candle, the photographs. All these objects can be displayed in a special place during the week before the family celebration. Invite the grandparents and godparents to come over for the evening. Parents can share the story of the baptism with each child: why their godparents were chosen;
who was present at the ceremony;
what the weather was like that day;
how the parents felt;
why the child was given his/her name.

Chapter 9

Celebrating the Seasons

Advent to Christmas
Christmas to Epiphany
Ash Wednesday to Easter
Easter to Pentecost

Advent To Christmas

Christmas is the celebration of the Gift of Emmanuel—God-in-this-world. The vibrancy and excitement of this precious gift is present to us only if we strive to help one another be aware of this in our community of faith. Celebrations recall root meanings and make truth present to us in a special way.

The "specialness" of Advent has always been that time spent waiting for the new presence of God at Christmas. The time we wait, then, is sacramental of the many occasions in life in which we must wait, yearn, and anticipate a new birth—the experience of encountering Jesus anew.

Keeping Advent in Your Home

Here are four things to decide first, for keeping Advent in your home:

1. During the week before Advent, get together and decide what your family will do together during Advent. Decide together. Plan realistically. Be selective and concentrate on doing one or two activities well.

2. Have a definite date and time to begin. The first Sunday of Advent is best. Begin with a special prayer as well as your decided activities.

3. Be committed to the family decision and make it a priority. The whole point is not to get so busy that Advent gets crowded out. Put it first.

4. Be careful not to let the Festival of Christmas interfere with the keeping of Advent.

A Family Advent Wreath

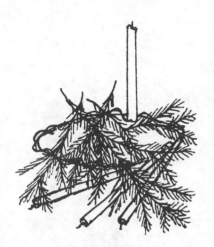

One of the best known customs for the season of Advent is the old German practice of the Advent Wreath. Although it has no direct liturgical significance, this wreath of evergreens with four purple candles (sometimes one is rose-colored) is rich in a symbolism which can make Advent more meaningful.

The *wreath* (a circle of evergreens) is a symbol of God and eternity—with no beginning and no end. The *evergreens' color* represents hope, the hope we all have of eternal life and of Christ's coming into our lives and of our accepting him more completely. The *four candles* represent the four weeks of Advent and the thousands of years that the world waited for the Redeemer. *Purple* is the ecclesiastical color of the season, symbolic of the work of conversion which we do to prepare our hearts for the coming of Jesus. *Candles* symbolize Christ the Light, who dispels the darkness by showing us the way.

Gather the family together on the Saturday evening before the first Sunday of Advent to assemble and bless the Advent Wreath. Explain the symbolism of each part of the wreath as the family puts it together.

The Blessing:

Parent: People waited for thousands of years for the Christ whom God had promised. Each year the Church uses the four weeks before Christmas to remember the long years of darkness when there wasn't Jesus. Our Advent wreath is a reminder to us that the birth of Jesus is Emmanuel, God-with-us, sharing our lives. His life is light to show us the way. It is also a reminder to us that we must work at preparing our hearts for Jesus to come into them once again.

All: O God, send your blessing upon our wreath and help us to understand its symbolism so that we might use it to help prepare our hearts for the coming of Christ.

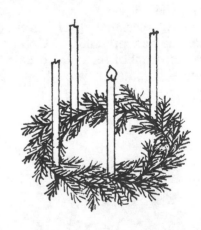

After the blessing, the presiding parent says the prayer for the first week of Advent and invites another member of the family to light the first candle. Each week a different prayer is said and another candle is lighted so that by the fourth week of Advent all the candles are burning brightly.

First Week: Lord, I know what it's like to want something and wait for it. I've wanted lots of things . . . and then after I got them I was happy for a little while, but, after all, they were just things and soon my happiness disappeared. Help me this Christmas, to want to be like Jesus, your son, so that instead of wanting and waiting for a lot of new things, I will be looking for ways to grow more loving, kind, and just. *All:* Amen.

Second Week: Lord, I believe that you have come into the world and that you want to come into my heart. I also believe that once I let you into my heart that you are present in the world today through me. Help me to remember to bring you wherever I go. *All:* Amen.

Third Week: Lord, I know that this is a season of hope. Help me to be the kind of person who radiates joy because I believe in your faithful presence. Give me hope and confidence in myself to go out and make your business my business. *All:* Amen.

Fourth Week: Lord, this year help me to do more than just sing all the familiar Christmas Carols; help me to live them. You sent Jesus as a bond of peace between us. May that peace on earth begin with me, and may joy in the world shine through us, as a family. *All:* Amen.

(These are only suggested prayers, you may want to express your own faith by composing your own prayers.)

On Christmas Eve with your family, renew the evergreens: add Christmas balls, and/or red and white carnations and replace the purple candles with white ones to symbolize Christ, the Light of the World who came to be with us. Or, use the idea of the Christ candle, also found in this section.

Family Advent Tree

Find a strong tree branch. Secure it in a pot of clay or sand, and cover the base with greens. Each day of Advent, spend a few moments with the scriptures and find a verse that speaks of the coming of the Christ or Messiah. Write the verse on a construction paper ornament (star, bell, etc.) Punch a hole in the ornament and run a piece of string or yarn through it. Each night, read the verse and then tie the verse/ornament to the tree.

The Jesse Tree

The *Jesse Tree* is a small evergreen tree or just a leafless branch on which symbols are placed which represent those who in the course of salvation history helped prepare the way for the Messiah or who were part of Christ's geneology. The symbols start at the bottom of the tree and progress in relative chronological order.

Children love the Christmas tree, and making a Jesse Tree at home helps calm the impatience for a Christmas tree. A good family project for the second Sunday of Advent would be to make the symbols and trim a Jesse Tree. Symbols can be made from construction paper, felt, contact or wrapping paper over cardboard forms or baker's dough. Make the Jesse Tree trimming a family ritual. Have members of the family make and hang one or more of the symbols and explain the symbol as they hang it on the tree. The ritual can be concluded with a prayer of blessing for the tree and the family by one of the parents. In the weeks that follow before Christmas, the family might spend time each day discussing the bible stories which correspond to the symbols on the tree.

The symbols for the Jesse Tree are many and varied, but the most usual are the following:

The *Apple* symbolizes Adam and Eve to whom the promise of the Messiah was first made. This was the beginning of our salvation history.

The *Altar of Sacrifice* symbolizes the story of Abraham and Isaac. God established a covenant with Abraham and his descendants. "I will make my covenant between you and me, and will give you many children," God told Abraham. "I will give you and your children this land in which you live, and I will be your God." So this was God's part of the bargain, and from the Chosen People God asked only love.

The *Ark*—The Chosen People were aware of the promise of the Messiah. They were also aware of the covenant of God to Abraham. For many years they kept the covenant faithfully. But as time went on, the people forgot the covenant and returned to evil ways. To remind them of their agreement, God sent a flood which destroyed all except the just man, Noah, and his family.

The *Coat of Many Colors* represents Joseph, the favorite son of Jacob, who was sold into slavery by his brothers, but who, like the Messiah, saved his brothers from death.

The people continued falling in and out of love with their God. To reestablish his covenant, God gave Moses *Tablets* of stone on which were written specific laws of love.

The *Key and the Crown* represent King David. The prophets told that the Messiah would be of the House of David. He would be the *Key* that opened heaven for all humankind.

A *scroll* can represent the numerous prophets who continually reminded the people of the Covenant Yahweh had made with them, and of the promise of the Messiah. It was through the prophets' tradition of constant correction and affirmation that there was a small remnant of people who accepted the Messiah.

The *Shell and Water* represented John the Baptist, the precursor of the Messiah and last of the Messianic prophets. John preached a baptism of repentance to help the people prepare for the Messiah.

St. Joseph, the foster father of Jesus, is represented by the *Hammer and Square* because he was a carpenter. Sometimes a *Donkey* is used to represent Joseph, because he led the donkey bearing Mary to Bethlehem.

The *Lily* is a symbol for Mary, the Mother of the Messiah.

The *Chi-Rho* (℞) is placed at the top of the tree to symbolize the Messiah or the Christ, the fulfillment of the promise and the "Desired one of all." *Chi* (×) and *Rho* (℘) are the first two Greek letters in the title *Christ. (Christ* is the Greek equivalent of the Hebrew title *Messiah,* meaning the Anointed One.)

Gift Certificate Tree

Children like to make presents for their families. A gift certificate or ticket tree is a simple way to inspire deeds of kindness as gifts children of any age can give.

Find a bare tree branch with several outgrowths. Secure it in a decorated tin can filled with clay or sand. During Advent, members of the family make specially shaped tickets for other members of the family and hang these tickets with yarn on the tree branches.

On one side of the ticket, print the recipient's name; on the opposite side, print something that you will *do* for that person, e.g., take the other person's turn at doing dishes, make someone's bed, take out the garbage, polish the other person's shoes, etc. The gift is actually given when the recipient returns the ticket to the one who gave it.

This idea shows that gift-giving is more than just a "Christmas thing" and also emphasizes that a true gift represents part of the giver.

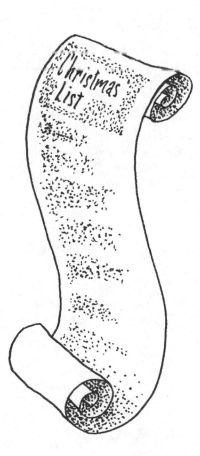

Life-Giving Gifts for the Christmas List

You might give similar gift certificates of service from your family to relatives, neighbors, friends. Sit down as a family and draw up your Christmas List—decide some personal way you might express the spirit of Christmas—giving the gift of self out of love. Design gift certificates indicating your family's gift. For example:

Dear _____,
    Our family's Christmas present is running errands that you will need on slippery, cold days—or any days. Just call us at _____ after school.
                                    Merry Christmas.

Here are a few other ideas, which have been adapted from *Major Feasts and Seasons* (see bibliography).

1. Give gifts of your own creating: candles, carving, needlepoint. Libraries and bookstores are loaded with books on crafts—even making things from junk.
2. Give a plant and directions for its care.
3. Give a service: a promise of so many hours of babysitting, a room painted, a garden planted, a car washed, a music lesson, an evening learning the names of the stars.
4. Give a gift of yourself: a story you have learned to tell, a dance or a song, a wonderful recipe.
5. Give parents or brothers and sisters something of the family: maybe a memento of some event.
6. Give a gift to the earth: begin to recycle all your paper, cans and bottles at a recycling center.
7. Donate money to a cause your friend is devoted to, and make the gift in the friend's name.
8. Save all your Christmas cards and send them back to the same people next year, asking them to do the same the following year, each time with a new date and message. It could be a real thing in ten years!
9. Loan your car to a carless person once a week for a month or two. Or, offer to drive someone to work with you.

St. Nicholas Day—December 6

Nicholas was a kindly and popular bishop who lived in the fourth century. Although he tried to perform his acts of kindness in secret, he became known for his generosity, taking care of orphans, giving dowries to poor servant girls, dropping money down chimneys for poor families to use, leaving food outside doors of hungry people. After his death, his kindnesses became legend in the minds and hearts of the needy. When he was declared a saint, his feastday was set on December 6, and the day became occasion for gift-giving, especially to children. Nicholas, himself, supposedly dispatched his gifts in shoes and stockings.

He is patron saint of Russia and Greece.

The idea of Santa Claus is often traced to St. Nicholas, but it is also mingled with a non-religious, Germanic legend about Thor, the kindly god of fire, who was associated with yule logs, fires and winter, and who rode in a chariot drawn by goats named Cracker and Gnasher. Custom in many European (and American) families is to have the children (big and small) leave their empty shoes outside their doors in hopes that some "unknown visitor" will fill them up, with oranges, apples, foil-covered chocolate "coins," or real ones, gifts given for no particular reason.

On December 5, the eve of St. Nicholas Day, explain the legend and follow through by having the children (and adults) put out shoes. Then, perhaps, each member of the family could decide on something to give away to someone else on December 6, not just because it's getting near the Christmas season, but because someone has need of what you have.

Origins of Christmas Traditions

The Date

The first reference to the feast of Christmas is found in the Roman Chronograph of 354 A.D., an almanac copied and illustrated by the Greek artist, Philocalus. This document contains a rudimentary Christian calendar in the form of two sets of dates.

At the head of the first set, for December 25, we find "Birth of Christ in Bethlehem of Judea." The date of December 25 was deliberately chosen at Rome sometime between 274 and 336 A.D. in order to counter the pagan feast of "Sol Invictus," the Unconquerable Sun, a feast which was officially instituted in 274 A.D. by the Emperor Aurelian.

From an anonymous treatise dating from the third or early fourth century, we read ". . . now they call this day the *Birthday of the Unconquerable!*" Who indeed is so unconquerable as our Lord, who overthrew and conquered death? And as for talking about the birthday of the Sun! He is the Sun of Justice! He whom the prophet Malachi said, "For you who fear my name there will arise the Sun of Justice, with healing in his wings."

The Paradise Tree

Hanging ornaments on trees seems to go all the way back to Roman times. Decorating a "Christmas Tree," however, seems to date from the 16th century in Germany. There, evergreen branches were freighted down with apples, sugar candy, and painted nuts. The inspiration for the "Christmas Tree" came from the medieval "mystery plays," performed in churches during the middle ages. A yearly favorite was an Advent performance called the "Paradise Play"—humankind's creation, expulsion from Eden, and promise of a savior. The only prop on stage was a fir tree, with apples suspended from its branches. Eventually the tree found its way into Christian homes. Later on, to point out to their children that the "paradise tree" was no longer a symbol of sin, but also a symbol of salvation, 16th century Germans combined it with another ancient symbol, the "Christmas Light." They also began to hang candies and cookies along side the "apples of sin" to symbolize the grace of "salvation." Thus, the "tree of sin," and the "light of Christ" grew into the *tree of light,* with its salvation-symbols. Today we all call it the "Christmas tree."

Christmas Cards

A little over 100 years ago, a wallpaper designer, Louis Prang of Boston, put on sale the first Christmas cards. However, the practice had been going on in England for at least 20 years before Prang. The first engraved Christmas card showed up in London in 1842. Today, over 5 billion cards bulge the postcarrier's bag each December. If you send Christmas cards, consider waiting until after Christmas, not only to give the postcarrier a break, but to allow Advent its own time and celebration.

The Christmas Creche

Creche is a French word meaning "cradle." It has been part of the Christmas tradition for over 750 years. The nativity scene was popularized as a Christmas custom by St. Francis of Assisi in 1224. St. Francis erected a manger and acted out the first Christmas with a cast of characters that included live animals and real people.

Home-Made Creche Figures

Making your own nativity figures for a creche can be both simple and enjoyable, and is an excellent way to review the Christmas story with children.

Collect all the pieces of cloth that have been stashed away for months. Make a water and flour solution (make it watery, not pastey). Use a styrofoam cone shape for the body of each figure; use an egg-shaped styrofoam ball for each head. Soak the pieces of material in the flour solution—*do not wring*. Then gently drape the wet material over the cone. This can be done in layers. Head pieces can be added, or decorative beads, sequins, etc. while the material is still wet, or they can be glued on after it has dried. Do not move the figures until the material is completely dry (usually 24 hours). The result is a creche unique to your family that can be used year after year.

"Magical" Mistletoe

Cutting of the mistletoe was once an occasion of great solemnity. Druid priests headed a stately procession into the forest to the site of the chosen oak. (Mistletoe grows on oak trees.) The Arch-Druid, robed all in white, climbed the tree and cut down the sacred vine with a golden sickle. Young maidens caught the mistletoe in a fair cloth, spread out below for that purpose. Then the mistletoe was divided, and each family bore home a sprig to hang over the door, for they believed that the powers of the plant to cure and to protect were very great. Indeed, according to legend, warring parties which met under mistletoe were said to have been overcome by its power, so that they would lay down their weapons and depart friends.

The English called the mistletoe "allheal"; the Welsh, "guidhel." Mistletoe later was used in Christian homes as a symbol of Christ, the Divine Healer. Today we kiss under the mistletoe.

Mexican Iluminada

The Mexican Iluminada is a simply made, inexpensive, energy-saving, yet attractive Christmas lawn decoration, as well as a meaningful custom.

The Iluminada consists of a medium-sized brown or other-colored bag with about an inch and a half of sand in the bottom. A votive-sized candle is set in the sand.

Instead of a paper bag you can make the Iluminada from a large juice can. Simply fill the cans with water, freeze, remove from freezer and with a nail and hammer "punch out" appropriate designs. After ice has melted and been emptied out, add sand or small stones and a votive candle as in bag.

Several of these are made to line the sidewalk and steps to the front door on Christmas Eve night as a sign of room and hospitality to Mary and Joseph, and to anyone who might be alone or traveling on this night.

As a parish project, each family can be invited to bring a "can" Iluminada to Mass on Christmas Eve to help light the way of welcome to the worshipping community.

The Christ Candle

The Christ Candle is a beautiful symbol of Jesus, the Light of the World. It is made by using a tall two-inch candle and decorating it with a Chi-Rho (☧) and other symbols of Christ made from tissue paper or painted on the candle with acrylics.

A good day to make the Christ Candle would be December 8, the Feast of the Immaculate Conception. When the decorating is completed, place the candle in a holder and cover it with a blue mantle, symbolic of Mary. On Christmas Day remove the mantle and light the candle.

The Miracle of the Poinsettia

The poinsettia was named after Dr. Joel Roberts Poinsett, who served as United States Ambassador to Mexico. Upon his return in 1829, he brought this flower with him to his home in South Carolina, where it flourished.

The people of Mexico call the poinsettia "The Flower of the Holy Night." According to a legend, on Christmas Eve long ago, a poor little boy went to church in great sadness, because he had no gift to bring to the Holy Child. He dared not enter the church; and kneeling humbly on the ground, he prayed and assured God how much he wanted to offer some lovely present. "But I am very poor and dread to approach you with empty hands." When he finally rose from his knees, there, springing up where his tears had fallen, was a green plant, with gorgeous blooms of dazzling red.

The poinsettia is today the traditional flower of Christmastide.

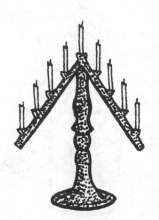

Celebrating Hanukkah

Like Christmas, Hanukkah has its origins in the change that happens to the sun during this season. And, like Christmas, Hanukkah has its historic occasion. In the second century before Jesus, the Jewish brothers Maccabees led a victorious guerilla revolt against the foreign occupiers of the land and were able to re-dedicate the temple in Jerusalem (the word *Hanukkah* means *dedication*).

The legend says that when the temple was recaptured, all of the sacred oil had been profaned except for a one day supply. It would take eight days to sanctify new oil. But a miracle happened and a tiny bit of holy oil burned for the whole eight days.

In the Jewish tradition, Hanukkah is a home festival. The simple observance of Hanukkah in the home can be occasion for a household to pray together.

A Simple Ritual for the Evenings of Hanukkah

The ritual calls for a nine-branched candleholder and 44 small candles (3½ inch birthday candles will work well). Make your own candelabra (called *menorah* in Hebrew) out of spools attached to a base, tinkertoys assembled in a variety of ways, clay, a piece of driftwood with nine holes drilled into it, etc.

Hanukkah lasts eight days: one candle is lighted the first day, two the second, etc. The ninth hole in the menorah is for the "servant candle" which lights the others each night. The reason for the small candles is that, by one custom, the lights are allowed to burn out each night. While this happens, nothing is done except to watch, to pray, and to enjoy the light, the darkness, and the quiet.

The Service

Light the "servant candle" and recite the blessings:

Blessed are you, Lord our God, ruler of the universe. You have given us life and permitted us to reach this season.

Blessed are you, Lord our God, ruler of the universe. You have sanctified us with your commandments and commanded us to kindle the light of Hanukkah.

Blessed are you, Lord our God, ruler of the universe. You performed miracles for our ancestors in those days, at this season.

Then the candle(s) are lighted and another member of the family says:

We kindle these lights on account of the miracles, wonders and deliverances which you performed for our ancestors. These lights are sacred throughout the eight days of Hanukkah; we are not permitted to make any use of them, but only to look at them, in order to give thanks to you.

A simple song after this would be good, e.g., a verse of *O Come, O Come, Emmanuel,* or *This Little Light of Mine,* or *Prepare Ye* from *Godspel.*

In silence let the candles burn out and then remain silent for a few moments in the dark.

Although not a usual part of the service, your family might wish to add a scripture reading each evening. The following schedule introduces a different prophet each evening and serves to bring a note of the Advent season into Hanukkah:

First night: *Amos* 5:14-15
Second night: *Hosea* 2:18-20
Third night: *Joel* 3:1-3
Fourth night: *Jeremiah* 33:14-16
Fifth night: *Isaiah* 7:14
Sixth night: *Ezekiel* 37:1-14
Seventh night: *Isaiah* 40:3-5
Eighth night: *Malachi* 3:1

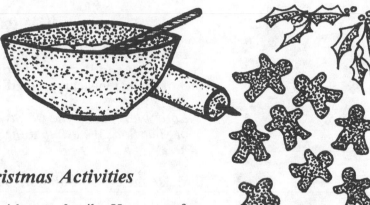

Modern-Day Pre-Christmas Activities

Begin some of your own traditions with your family. Here are a few examples:

Shopping for Fun

Take the whole family to a shopping center, not to buy anything, but just for fun. Watch the people. Look at the decorations. What are people buying? What are their moods? How many are using credit cards? What is the most unusual thing that you see? Do some people look like Scrooge? Are children's eyes bigger and brighter than usual?

On the way home stop somewhere for hot chocolate and talk over what each in the family has observed and share reactions.

Christmas Goodies

How long has it been since Dad or the boys helped cook? Choose a baking day in which everyone participates. Everyone likes to eat Christmas goodies; and while the family is busy baking together, you can have a family caroling session.

Television Party

Even though many people are unhappy with the quality of television programming, there are some exceptionally good opportunities. Why not check the TV schedule in search of a Christmas special the family can view together? Plan popcorn or something special for the evening.

Christmas to Epiphany

Christmas Eve Prayer Service

The whole family might plan this special service of hymns, scripture readings and prayers for Christmas Eve. It is not difficult to choose appropriate readings and songs for this occasion. The service might take place just before opening gifts or after dinner.

Blessing The Creche

In a small procession each household member can carry one of the creche figures to its place of honor. When all the figures are in place, one of the parents can proceed with the prayer of blessing:

Lord, bless this creche we have prepared in remembrance of the birth of your Son. We ask that the light of his goodness shine on all of us here.

Sprinkle the creche with holy water; incense may also be used.

Blessing for the Tree

Lord, we ask your blessing upon this tree. May its ever-greenness be a sign in our lives of the hope of the Christmas season, its glittering ornaments a sign of the joy of the Christmas season, and the gifts beneath it a sign of the love of the Christmas season.

Sprinkle the tree with holy water. Conclude this little ritual by bringing its significance home to the present day. Discuss the following questions with one another:

"What if Jesus were born now? How would the holy family look?"
"Where would the baby be born? Think of the places that would be like Bethlehem—no room, a stable and a manger."
"Imagine who would be like angels, shepherds, sheep, the Wise Men."
"Are there people as evil and powerful as King Herod and his counselors? Who are they?"

Blessing of the Christmas Dinner

If you already have a tradition for blessing this meal, then by all means continue it. If you do not, the following may help you get started.

The stuff of which this blessing is made is the love that went into the selection and preparation of the food, the generosity of those who labored that such food might be purchased, the beauty of the table which has been set, perhaps the labor of making special place markers. But most of all, the blessing is in the fellowship of the table, the gathering itself, and the time we take for this. Let nothing be hurried. The blessing begins when all have assembled at the table. The ringing of a small jingle bell might call everyone to silence. Then in silence the oldest child lights the candles. When they are burning, one of the adults prays:

For the wonder of birth, we thank you, God. And for this day to celebrate the birth of Jesus at Bethlehem, the House of Bread. We sing then with the angels, with the cattle and the sheep, with the shepherds and the stars of Heaven, with Joseph and Mary:

All join hands and sing: *O Come Let Us Adore Him! O Come Let Us Adore Him! O Come Let Us Adore Him, Christ the Lord.*

The leader continues after all have taken their glasses (of water, wine, milk, or whatever) and are holding them for a toast:

May your blessing, O God, be upon all creation. May the earth that brought forth this food be blessed, and all of us and so become the first banquet of this holy season, may the sharing of the meal show forth the sharing which happened at Bethlehem when in Jesus' birth we share with You Your own holiness.

Then all say a "Merry Christmas" and drink together. This blessing might be used for festive meals throughout the Christmastime: simply add in the first prayer . . . *The birth of Jesus at Bethlehem, the House of Bread, and the holiness of his friend, John the apostle . . .* or *. . . and the glory of his manifestation to the Magi. . . .*

Keeping Christmas

Rituals for the Twelve Days After Christmas

How has it ever happened that Christmas can be over and gone, totally wiped out, by the morning of December 26? Or even by the morning of December 25 in some cases?

Christmas is a *season,* not just a day. It is a season which lasts at least 12 days, and until February 2 on the Church's liturgical calendar. In fact, in most European countries the gift-giving aspect of the season takes place on Epiphany, the Feast of the Magi's visit when Jesus' birth was revealed to the Gentile (non-Jewish) nations. December 25 is reserved for the celebration of Christ's birth. It might be good for us to save some of our gift-giving for Epiphany, since Christmas so often seems to end when the last package is unwrapped.

We need to make the Christmas season a festival, a time when business-as-usual stops, a time when we tell special stories. Now the story of Christmas is the most out-of-the-ordinary story of a birth. But like all good stories, this birth story surrounds itself with other stories that seem to overflow. If we are to make Christmas a season, then we need to pace the story, and that is the purpose of this section of the book.

If we believe there is a reason for festivity, then *we* make the festival by being willing to take the time and energy to do the unusual; for example, leave your tree up until January 6 (Epiphany), go caroling on the feast of St. Stephen (December 26), etc.

As with your Advent planning, gather the household together for Christmas planning, remembering, futuring. Encourage children to recall and tell what they remember about past Christmases. What was most fun, exciting, beautiful? Parents too recall sad times, high points, customs, foods. How did the grandparents celebrate Christmas? What has changed? stayed the same? What about Christmas this year? What's good and holy? What's bad and selfish? How shall we celebrate it? Make a short list of suggestions (things to keep, things to drop, things to leave the same); look at them again on Epiphany, and the next year. See if you feel the same.

A New Year's Custom

A New Year's custom that deserves ritual is taking this day to visit friends: old friends and new, announced and unannounced visits. Bring along a big bag of nuts (some will think that appropriate for anyone who would not spend New Year's before the TV) and share with your friends and with those you meet on the way (try walking!)

(Adapted from *Major Feasts and Seasons.* Vol. 2, No. 1)

An Epiphany Celebration

January 6 is the day we celebrate the Magi finally reaching the creche. Until that time, children can have great fun moving them a few inches across the room until the great day that they arrive, and Christ is made manifest to the Gentiles.

Have the children help make a "crown cake" (bundt cakes can give the illusion of a crown topped with frosting and gum-drop jewels). This will help the family to see that the gifts brought by the Magi (who were astrologers of sorts) were recognizing Christ's kingship.

An evening re-enactment of the story of the Magi can also be a most enjoyable experience, since children love to dramatize things. To begin the enactment, someone can read the scripture account of Jesus' manifestation (*Matthew* 2:1-12). Then have family members assume the roles of Herod, the Magi (it is not necessary to have exactly three, since there probably were not three; there may have been two, six, or any number of them.) They meet and talk to Herod and finally reach Bethlehem where Mom, Dad and the baby of the family (Jesus was probably two years old), or a doll, are playing the roles of Mary, Joseph and Jesus. The gifts presented might be resolutions written on paper in boxes beautifully wrapped as gifts. When the dramatization is over, share the ''crown cake'' together.

The Epiphany Blessing of the Home

When we bless, we praise and thank God for a person or an object. And we pray that God's care surround what we are blessing: ''May God hold you in the palm of his hand . . .'' as the Irish blessing has it.

Epiphany is traditionally the day when homes are blessed. Those who live in a house join together for the blessing.

Process through every room. Everyone involved may carry something: candles, incense, holy water, a crucifix, the symbols of the Magi (gold, incense, myrrh). In each room one person asks the blessing with something as simple as, *May this room be blessed in the name of the Father and of the Son and of the Holy Spirit.*

Holy water is sprinkled, the corners are incensed, and anyone can wish a blessing on what happens in that room, *May this bedroom be filled with sweet rest and good dreams! May this basement stay dry and cool! May this kitchen be fragrant for all who work here.*

Sometimes it is customary to carry chalk and mark each door with the year and the initials of the Magi (Caspar, Melchior, Balthazar); crosses separate the letters and numbers: 19 + C + M + B + 80.

In conclusion, pray:

Visit this home, we ask you, O Lord. Chase far away from it all the snares of the enemy. Send your Holy Spirit to live with us and keep us at peace. May your blessings be always upon us.

Today concludes the Christmas Festival. The final celebration is to take down the tree and decorations. The house is back to normal. But normal for a household is not ''the same as before''—not if the Festival has been kept with heart and soul and body. Those who come out of a festival are not quite those who went in.

Ash Wednesday to Easter

Lenten Activities at Home

Lent is a time of prayer, penance and sacrifice, a time for the entire family to be more attentive to the words of Jesus and a time to try harder to put his teachings into practice. It is a time of concentrated effort toward the springtime of spiritual growth, of rebirth and renewal.

However, the perennial problem in families seems to be: How can our children best experience the 40 days of Lent? How can they learn the real meaning of sacrifice?

Following are a number of activities you might try to aid in an experiential celebration of the season and a means whereby the problem might begin to be worked out for your family. You may wish to choose one or more of the suggestions.

Forty days is a very long time for children. To have Lent become more meaningful for them, take one week and perhaps one activity at a time. However, family prayer could be continued throughout the season and after.

Regarding sacrifice, a child is capable of real sacrifice, but the beauty of such sacrifice is its spontaneity; at such times one feels the Spirit of God at work. To suggest that a child "give something up" or do something nice for someone because it pleases Jesus actually tampers with his or her early moral development. If the child would like to do something kind for someone, that is *sufficient in itself* as an act that makes the child more Christ-like and as an attempt to follow the teaching of the Gospel. Lent is a journey *with* Jesus, not *for* him.

An Ash Wednesday Family Service

Seasons like Lent need a definite beginning. All good resolutions go into effect today. If the whole family can't get to the church for ashes, have a prayer service at home. Ashes can be made out of things or symbols of things that you want to bring under control in your life, e.g., money, faults written on paper, etc.

Gather the family together, read and discuss *Joel* 2:12-18 or *Matthew* 6:1-6; 16-18. Allow a few minutes for thought during which each member of the family decides which faults will be worked on. These are written on a small piece of paper, crumpled and placed in a brazier to be burned with last year's palm branch. You might also cut a hunk of hair from each head to be burned. Set a fire and watch as a part of you is turned quickly to ashes. As the fire burns, the parent says: *Lord have mercy on us, forgive us, and help us to do better in the future.* Then stand in silence until the flame dies out.

While the contents of the brazier are cooling, the family might discuss the meaning of Lent and what each person or the household as a whole is going to do to grow during the season.

When the ashes are cool, the oldest takes some and marks the forehead of the next oldest saying: *Repent and receive the Good News . . .* and so through the entire family until the youngest marks the oldest. The service can be concluded with a song or prayer together.

A Lenten Journey Of Love

We are a pilgrim people, and while Lent is a good time to look back on where we have been, more importantly, we look ahead toward where we are going. This *Journey of Love* may be an aid. It was originated several years ago by the pastor of the First Christian Church in Oklahoma City. For each of the six weeks of Lent, there are specific aspects of daily loving.

First Week: *The Hand of Love.* Write a letter a day to a friend near or far away and tell him/her how much you appreciate their friendship.

Second Week: The Voice of Love. Phone two or three people just to say what they mean to you or to say "Thank you" or "I'm sorry." Call people you've intended to phone but somehow never have. Remember, love and gossip don't go together.

Third Week: *The Deed of Love.* Take something you have made or bought to two or three friends who mean much to you, but for whom you rarely express your love—a pie, a plant, a birdhouse, a small remembrance that has your love as a wrapping.

Fourth Week: The Heart of Love. Make a list of ten people for whom you will pray daily. Include your friends, your enemies, those you don't like. Forgive them if they have wronged you, and ask forgiveness if you have wronged them.

Fifth Week: *The Mind of Love.* Use this week to pray for yourself and look inward. Read the Gospel according to John. Plan during the week to do a little extra meditating and praying in a quiet place, such as a church.

Sixth Week: *The Victory of Love.* This is the week of celebration. God's love for us is revealed in many ways. Get out of doors and breathe in the air of spring. Fly a kite. Have your friends in for dinner or a party. Let your joy be full with life abundant in faith, hope and love.

This little plan for Lent could well find us at Easter, a "new creation." And some, if not all, our faults could well turn to ashes and dust as we are reminded on Ash Wednesday. Their ash becomes a sign of victory through forgiveness. It is a journey of love which may entail some pain and difficulty—but aren't these basic ingredients of loving?

Lenten Calendar

Make an appropriately decorated calendar of the 40 days of Lent by superimposing two pieces of heavy paper. For each day have a flap that opens onto the back sheet to reveal an activity for the family for that day. For example: reading a particular bible story, praying a decade of the rosary, visiting a nursing home, sharing cookies or cake with a neighbor, sharing allowances, fasting at one meal and giving the money saved to the social action fund or some other charity, etc.

For Under 18 Only

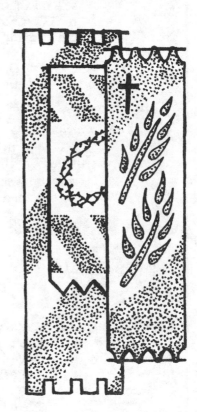

Lent means *doing something* more than *giving up* something. Is there something from the following list that you could try to *do* during Lent, completely on your own, without your parents "making you" do it?

You know that neighbor on the block whom no one likes? Find a way to be friendly. (OK. No one said this was going to be easy.)
Read a bedtime story to your younger brothers and sisters.
Shovel walks for someone who can't—without pay.
Visit a lonely oldster.
Listen to someone you don't enjoy.
Be a peacemaker with a younger brother or sister.
Give Mom a hug when she's having a bad day.
Smile more often to let others know that you want to share your happiness.
Babysit for a mother who doesn't get out very often—without pay.
Show your understanding side to a friend who is having a bad day.
Teach a younger family member a new game, or play an old game with them.
Make banners to remind the family that Easter is coming.
Take a walk with someone in your family after supper or on a weekend.
Read to a blind person.
Add an extra "I love you" to your daily conversation at home.
(Adapted in part from a column by Dolores Curran)

Goodbye to Alleluia

By ancient custom, the *Alleluia* is not spoken or sung during Lent. Some say that's silly: it's just a word in Hebrew that means "Praise the Lord!" We say it in English, why not in Hebrew? But *Alleluia* is more than a word. It's part of who we are. Our ancestors in the faith have shouted it since long before Jesus.

At one time, it was customary for Christians to bury the *Alleluia* before Lent. We can revive the practice. With another family or two form a procession, carrying spades, an empty wooden box, a beautiful *Alleluia* on paper (made by the children). Go to the largest snowdrift in the yard (the one that will melt the slowest) and dig a deep grave, then sing a last, most enthusiastic *Alleluia*. The written *Alleluia* is then placed in its coffin and buried as everyone takes a turn throwing on snow. Then join hands and pray for a good Lent and that all other seeds to be buried in weeks ahead will sing their *Alleluias*. The *Alleluia* is raised on Easter with song and flowers.

(from *Major Feasts and Seasons*, Vol. 1, No. 2)

The Waiting Table

Watching and waiting are other characteristics of Lent—for the new life of spring. For Easter when we commemorate Christ's Resurrection, and the special time when we can celebrate our new life in Baptism. It is also a time of interior activity and growth.

Begin with a special trip to the store to find some purple material (purple is a Lenten color) to be hemmed for a tablecloth. The scriptures are placed in the center of the table. As Lent progresses, the table can be decorated first with dormant branches; then as the first signs of spring begin to show themselves, the branches can be replaced with daffodils, tulips, pussy willows, or lilac branches.

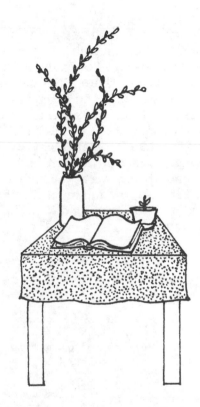

You might also experiment with indoor growing projects which the children can watch. Mustard, bean, wheat or marigold seeds work well, as do sweet potatoes or carrot tops. As time goes on, children will begin to find objects which to them are symbolic of waiting for spring, and of the death-to-life activity taking place within nature.

Pictures depicting the events of Palm Sunday, Holy Thursday, and Good Friday, either drawn by the children or commercial pictures can be added at the appropriate times to depict Jesus' journey from death to new life. Pictures and mementos of the children's baptisms can also be added after a discussion of how Lent was a special time for the early Christians to prepare for their baptism, which was conferred at the Easter Vigil Service.

For Easter, the tablecloth is changed to white. An Easter Candle is decorated with symbols of spring and Easter or with the symbols that are on the Paschal candle at church and given the place of honor next to the scriptures on the table, representing the Light of Christ Risen. Flowers, Easter eggs, butterflies, stuffed bunnies and chicks, and other symbols of spring and Easter can surround the candle and bible.

(Adapted from *Religion Teacher's Journal*)

Personalized Cross

Make either a wooden cross (out of sticks or boards) or a paper cross to be tacked on the wall. Have each member of the family trace his/her hand on construction paper, cut it out and write on it something special that s/he would like to do during Lent (these can be changed weekly). The hands are then placed on the cross as a reminder. On Holy Saturday, remove the hands and replace them with tissue or crepe paper flowers to show that the efforts to be better Christians during Lent turned into something beautiful, as did the glorious cross of Christ on the Resurrection.

Pretzel Prayer Reminders

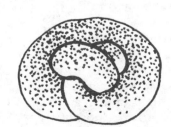

Making pretzels is an ancient Lenten custom. Legend has it that one day a monk who made altar breads found himself with leftover dough. He shaped the dough into the form of dolls with arms crossed in prayer, went out into the streets and gave them to the children to remind them to pray. The breads were called "bracellae" which means "little arms."

From this Latin word, the Germans later coined the word "pretzel." Lent is a time of prayer. And the pretzel is a reminder. How about the family making pretzels together during Lent?

Popcorn Project

A paper cup with appropriate Lenten or spring decorations is placed in a special place, accessible to all. Next to it is a jar of popcorn kernels. Each day, each member of the family decides upon something to work on for that day. For example: trying to use the gift of their hands to help others, to share with others and to take care of things. The gift of ears to listen better to others; the gift of eyes to see the needs of others, to see the beauty of all God's creation and to keep their eyes on their own work. The gift of speech to thank God for God's many gifts, to be quiet at times so that others are able to learn or pray, to speak loudly enough so that others may hear, to speak only kindly of others, etc. At the end of each week, the kernels can be popped and shared. Watching the kernels grow and burst and change can be a good symbol of how the little things done each day can bring about a growth in the Christ Life within us.

Progressive Butterfly Banner

The butterfly is an ancient Easter symbol. To visualize the Lenten experience of death-resurrection, try a progressive butterfly banner. Just as the butterfly which emerges from the cocoon is the same caterpillar in new form, so Jesus, emerging from the tomb is the same person—glorified.

Take a piece of felt or large poster paper. Each week, add one part to the poster as follows: 1. a bare branch with a caption such as *Life Through Death;* 2. a cocoon on the branch; 3. a head is added to the cocoon which now becomes the body of the butterfly; 4. legs are added; 5. eyes are added to the head; 6. three-dimensional wings are added to complete the Easter poster. Adding to the poster can be done as part of your family prayer.

Family Food Box

At the end of dinner, there's a brief discussion about the next day's dinner menu. The cook tells what's planned. Then one of the family (depending on whose turn it is) decides which item on the menu to eliminate. The money that item would cost is then put in the family food box to be used to buy food for the hungry. For example, on the day spaghetti, salad and garlic bread are on the menu, the one whose turn it is to eliminate an item suggests, ''Let's not have meat in the spaghetti sauce'' and into the food box goes $2.50.

At the end of the Lenten season, contribute the money to a cause of justice or mercy.

Passover Meal at Home

Celebrate a family Passover meal and enable the family to experience the relationship between our Jewish and Christian ritual heritage. Passover usually coincides with Holy Week. Holy Thursday would be a good day to have a family Passover, with a follow-up experience of the celebration of the institution of the Eucharist. You may also wish to invite another family to celebrate with you.

Sometime during Lent, the story of the Israelites' exile, slavery and liberation should be read or told with an explanation of the celebration of Passover as a Thanksgiving feast celebrated annually in honor of their freedom. Both Passover for the Jews and Easter for Christians recognize that all things come from God: light, bread, wine, freedom—all good things. The Jewish prayers are prayed in a spirit of thanksgiving and blessing, as are the Eucharistic prayers. The Exodus celebrates the Chosen People's freedom from oppression. Each Jew is to become aware of this personally at each Passover. For the Christian, the Paschal season celebrates redemption from the effects of sin by Christ's passion and resurrection, and God's gift of grace, especially through Holy Communion. Both are rooted in history and scripture to show God's fulfillment of God's plan of salvation.

Passover Meal

The following is designed to assist you with the planning, preparation, and celebration of the Passover or Paschal Meal. The Passover Meal itself will run well over an hour, so plan to set aside a good portion of the evening for it. Members of the group who will be sharing the meal should be involved in the preparation of the meal. This will probably mean that you will want to begin early with preparations, even a day or two in advance.

PREPARATION:

1. *House Cleaning:* Members of the family join in the task of housecleaning. On the afternoon or the day before the meal, have several members clean the area(s) to be used for the meal. The setting up of tables and chairs, plates, cups, etc. is all a part of this housecleaning ritual and should be part of the day's preparation.
2. *Decorations:* This ritual meal is rich with symbolism; ideas for decorations are unlimited. Table decorations, centerpieces, wall hangings, place cards, and many other items can be made by the family based upon the predominant symbols of the ritual. The making of such decoration can be part of the afternoon or week's preparations and will serve to enhance the ritual meal.

To add to the solemnity of the meal, participants can dress up in formal attire for the meal.

3. *The Passover Foods: The Menu*

Roast Lamb—to symbolize the sacrificial lamb offered by the Israelites and eaten on the eve of their departure from Egypt; in the Christian tradition, the Lamb of God becomes a symbol for Jesus Christ.

Matzos—to symbolize the unleavened bread the Jews ate when they
were freed from Egypt. Available at the market. It can also be made
using the following recipe:

> 3 cups whole wheat or rye flour
> 1 tsp. salt
> 1 tblsp. brown sugar or honey
> 1 ¼ cup sour milk
> 1 egg
> ½ cup melted butter
> 1 tblsp. baking powder
> Roll out ½ inch flat with rolling pin or hands on a floured surface
> and make into round forms.
> Bake: 425° for 15 minutes.

Bitter Herbs—to symbolize the bitterness of slavery and addictions.
Use horseradish or spring radishes.

Greens—As a token of gratitude to God for the products of the
earth. Use parsley and/or watercress or endive.

Salt Water—A dip for the greens and bitter herbs.

Haroses—to symbolize the mortar which the Hebrew slaves used in
their servitude. A mixture of chopped apples, chopped nuts, cinna-
mon and wine (this may be prepared like a fruit salad or chopped in a
blender).

Wine—to symbolize the blood marking the doorposts of the Jews so
that the avenging angel would passover them. In Christian tradition,
we commemorate the blood of Christ shed in his passion. Use preferably a red wine.

Additional Foods:

The traditional Passover menu may be supplemented with other
foods to "fill out" the meal. Some possibilities are rice, a vegetable
or green salad, and perhaps a cake for dessert. (A white coconut cake
in the shape of a lamb would be very appropriate.)

If additional foods are to be used, they should not be present at the
table until the ritual meal has been eaten. The traditional Passover
foods (above menu) should be present on the table from the beginning of the ritual (some lamb may be kept warm—the bone and small
pieces may be on the table prior to the meal). These traditional foods,

however, should not be consumed until the appropriate time in the ritual.

Notes on Passover Foods:

1. Be sure that enough of the Passover foods are available. When the ritual calls for the eating or drinking of a food, only a small portion need be taken by each person. The remainder of the food can be saved for later in the meal after the ritual section.

2. If young people are present, you may wish to dilute the wine with water, cherry kool-aid, or soda.

3. The ceremonial cups of wine may be served in one of two ways:

Each person has his/her own glass of wine or one large cup is used from which all can drink.

Additional Notes:

1. Please go through the ritual carefully before the meal so that you are familiar with the order of events, with pronunciation of words and with phrasing. It is advisable to practice by reading aloud one's part in the ritual.

2. Feel free to make your own personal additions as you see appropriate for your group. But be sure to retain the significance of this very special meal.

3. Readers are needed for these reading parts: *Mother, Leader, Father, Child.*

The Ritual

I. INTRODUCTORY BLESSINGS

All gather around the table and stand quietly. The mother lights the candles and says the following traditional prayer of the mother in the Jewish family as she lights the festival day candle before the meal:

Mother: Blessed are you, O Lord God, King of the universe, who has sanctified us by your commandments and has commanded us to light the festival lights. Blessed are you, O Lord God, King of the universe, who has kept us alive and sustained us and brought us to this season. May our home be consecrated, O God, by the light of your countenance, shining upon us in blessing and bringing us peace.

Leader: This is Holy Week, a time that joins for us the Old and the New Covenant. At this season, the Jewish people celebrate the feast of the Passover or Pasch. More than 1400 years before the time of Jesus the Christ, the chosen people were suffering in slavery in Egypt. God raised up Moses as their leader, and Moses tried to secure their release from captivity. Despite the hardships of nine successive plagues which God sent to them, the Egyptian pharoah still refused the pleas of Moses to set his people free. Then an angel of the Lord was sent to strike down the first-born son of every Egyptian family, but at God's command, each Jewish family had sacrificed a lamb and sprinkled its blood on the doorposts. And the angel, seeing the blood, passed over their homes and their children were spared.

Then, finally, the pharoah permitted the Jews to leave because he feared further punishment. They fled in haste, to wander amid the hardships in the desert for 40 years before coming to the promised land of Israel. And God commanded Moses that the Jews should make a remembrance of their day of deliverance. Thus the Passover became the great feast of sacrifice, of deliverance and of thanksgiving. Each Passover meal revolves around the retelling (the *Haggadah*) of this providential act (see *Exodus* 12).

We who are the followers of Christ see the working of God's concern for the people of God. As God sent Moses to rescue the Israelites from captivity in Egypt, so God lovingly sent Jesus to lead humankind from slavery and sin. Through his life, death and resurrection Christ enables us to enter life with God.

At this time Christians and Jews celebrate their own feasts in their own ways and we can see in these celebrations the common bond of the symbolism of the Exodus. Jesus was a Jew and today we wish to draw upon the traditional Jewish Seder and the words of the New Testament to help us more fully appreciate Jesus' observance of his Jewish heritage, whose laws and rituals he kept.

Matthew's, Mark's and Luke's accounts of Jesus' passion and death for us each begin with his celebration of the Paschal meal:

> "Now on the first day of Unleavened Bread the disciples came to Jesus to say, 'Where do you want us to make the preparations for you to eat the Passover?' " (*Matthew* 26:17; *Mark* 14:12; *Luke* 22:7-9)

II. INTRODUCTORY HALLEL: PSALMS OF PRAISE

Leader: In the Passover feast, before the meal is eaten, the first psalms of the *Hallel*—the hymns of praise which the Jews recited at the great feast— are recited. We will alternate in reading the verses.

Psalm 113

> *Men & Boys:* Alleluia!
> You servants of Yahweh, praise,
> Praise the name of Yahweh!
> Blessed be the name of Yahweh,
> Henceforth and forever!
> From east to west,
> Praised be the name of Yahweh!

Women & Girls: High over all nations,
Yahweh's glory transcends the heavens!
Who is like Yahweh our God?
Enthroned so high, Yahweh needs to stoop
To see the sky and earth!

Men & Boys: Yahweh raises the poor from the dust;
Lifts up the needy from the dunghill
To give them a place with princes,
With the princes of Yahweh's people.
Yahweh enthrones the barren woman in her house
by making her the happy mother of sons and daughters.

Psalm 114

Women & Girls: Alleluia!
When Israel came out of Egypt,
            the House of Jacob from a foreign nation,
And Israel from Egypt's domain,

Men & Boys: The sea fled at the sight,
The Jordan stopped flowing,
The mountains skipped like rams,
And the hills like lambs.

Women & Girls: Sea, what makes you run away?
Jordan, why stop flowing?
Why skip like rams, you mountains,
Why like lambs, you hills?

Men & Boys: Quake, earth, at the coming of your Master,
At the coming of the God of Jacob,
Who turns rocks into pools,
Flint into fountains.

III. TRADITIONAL PASSOVER PRAYERS

Leader: The first act of the Jewish Passover is a benediction, the *Kiddush*. The Father takes up a cup of wine and recites this blessing:

Father: Blessed are you, O Lord our God, King of the universe, Creator of the fruit of the vine. Blessed are you, O Lord our God, King of the universe, who has chosen us among all peoples and sanctified us with your commandments. In love you have given us, O Lord our God, solemn days of joy and festive seasons of gladness, even this day of the feast of the unleavened bread, a holy convocation, a memorial of the departure from Egypt. You have chosen us for your service and have made us sharers in the blessing of your holy festivals. Blessed are you, O Lord our God, who has preserved us, sustained us, and brought us to this season.

(All take up their cups)

Leader: We who are Christians know, as Luke writes (22:18) that on the night Jesus celebrated the Pasch with his disciples, he said:

> "From now on, I tell you, I shall not drink wine until the kingdom of God comes."

(All drink of the wine)

Leader: The next traditional act of the Jewish Passover meal is eating the greens. The greens are a symbol that nature comes to life in springtime. Following Jewish custom, we dip the greens in salt water and pray:

Father: Blessed are you, O Lord our God, King of the universe, Creator of the fruit of the earth.

(All eat of the greens dipped in salt water.)

Leader: Another action of the Jewish Passover meal is breaking the matzo. The Father lifts up the matzo and says:

Father: Lo, this the bread of affliction which our fathers and mothers ate in the land of Egypt. Let all who are hungry come and eat. Let all who are in want come and celebrate the Passover with us. May it be God's will to redeem us from all trouble and from all servitude. Next year at this session may the whole house of Israel be free.

(The father replaces the matzo on its plate.)

IV. THE QUESTIONS

Leader: At the ancient Passover meal, the youngest child asked the father four traditional questions about the Passover. In time, in order to carry on the discussion about the symbolic foods, other questions were also asked about their meanings. In more recent times, the same four questions have been asked at the *Seder*. The questions we ask tonight are similar but have been adapted to bring to mind the relationships between the Hebrew and Christian Testaments.

Child: Why is this night different from all other nights?

Father: In the *Mishnah* we find the ancient teaching of the Jews concerning the meaning of the Passover meal:

> "In every generation a person must so regard self as if he or she came forth out of Egypt, for it is written: 'And you shall tell your children in that day saying: It is because of that which the Lord did for me when I came forth out of Egypt.' (*Exodus* 13:8) Therefore are we bound to give thanks, to praise . . . and to bless Yahweh who wrought all these wonders for our fathers and mothers and for us. Yahweh brought us out from bondage to freedom, from sorrow to gladness, and from mourning to a festival day, and from darkness to great light, and from servitude to redemption: so let us lay before Yahweh the *Hallel,* our song of

praise." We who are followers of Jesus know that as God rescued the Israelites through Moses from the slavery of Egypt, so God called us through Christ to leave our slavery to sin. Christ passed from this world to his Father, showing us the way and preparing a place for us, as he said:

> "No one can come to the Father except through me." (*John* 14:6)

Paul tells us in his letter to the Church at Corinth:

> "And for anyone who is in Christ, there is a new creation; the old creation has gone, and now the new one is here." (*II Corinthians* 5:17)

And again he wrote:

> "Now, however, you have been set free from sin, you have been made slaves of God, and you get a reward leading to your sanctification and ending in eternal life. For the wage paid by sin is death; the gift given by God is eternal life in Christ Jesus our Lord." (*Romans* 6:22-33)

Child: Why do we eat bitter herbs tonight at the special meal?

Father: The Jews of old ate bitter herbs on Passover night, as do the Jews today, because "our ancestors were slaves in Egypt and their lives were made bitter." We who are followers of Jesus the Christ do not hesitate to taste of this bitterness as a reminder of his passion and death or to recall that he said:

> "Anyone who does not carry his or her cross and come after me cannot be my disciple." (*Luke* 14:27)

(All eat a bitter herb)

Child: Why do we eat herbs tonight, and this time with sweet jam?

Father: We dip the bitter herbs into the *haroses,* sweet jam, as did the Jews of old, as a sign of hope. Our ancestors were able to withstand the bitterness of slavery because it was sweetened by the hope of freedom. We who are followers of Christ are reminded that by sharing in the bitterness of Christ's sufferings we strengthen our hope. Paul writes in his letter to the Church in Rome:

> "It is by faith and through Jesus that we have entered this state of grace in which we can boast about looking forward to God's glory. But that is not all we can boast about; we can boast about our sufferings. These sufferings bring patience, as we know; and patience brings perseverance, and perseverance brings hope, and this hope is not deceptive, because the love of God has been poured into our hearts by the Holy Spirit which has been given us." (*Romans* 5:2-5)

Christ and his disciples—and all Jews who celebrate the Passover—tell the *Haggadah* during the Paschal meal. *Haggadah* means "retelling." It is the retelling of the Israelites' salvation from the tenth plague because the lintels of their doors had been marked with the blood of the lamb sacrificed at God's command and of the story of the exodus of the Jews from Egypt.

The yearly retelling of the deliverance of the Jews is an essential act in the Passover meal. As the evidence of God's loving care is refreshed in the minds of each individual each year, so is the renewal of their dependency upon God for all things, particularly their freedom from slavery.

(All dip a second bitter herb in haroseth and eat it.)

Child: Why did the Jews at the time of Jesus eat the Paschal Lamb when they celebrated the Passover meal?

Father: At the time of the liberation from Egypt, at God's command each family took a lamb, sacrificed it, ate it, and sprinkled its blood on the doorpost and lintel. And on that night, seeing the blood, the angel of the Lord passed over them, killing the Egyptians and sparing the Israelites. The Jews continued a memorial sacrifice of the lamb in the Temple for each family in Jerusalem at the time of the Passover. The lamb was brought home, roasted and eaten in a memorial meal. Since the destruction of the Temple in Jerusalem, there is no longer sacrifice but the meaning of the Paschal Lamb is retold by Jewish people today.

Followers of Jesus the Christ know that he is our Lamb, who sacrificed himself for us, and by his death and resurrection, enabled us to pass with him into eternal life with God. As Paul says:

> "Christ our Passover has been sacrificed." (*I Corinthians* 5:7)

(All eat a piece of the lamb.)

Child: Why did Christ and his disciples wash at table?

Father: At the festival table of the Jews it is customary to wash the hands of all present while saying this prayer:

> "Blessed are you, O Lord our God, King of the universe, who sanctified us with your commandments and commanded us concerning the washing of hands."

On this night followers of Christ are taught a new meaning. Jesus, while washing the feet of his disciples, taught his commandment of love and service for others:

> "The greatest among you must be servant. Anyone who exalts self will be humbled, and anyone who humbles self will be exalted." (*Matthew* 23:11)

Child: Why did Jesus and his disciples eat unleavened bread at the Passover meal?

Father: The blessing and the breaking of the matzo is one of the important parts of the feast of the Pasch. The origin of the matzo was this:

> "When Pharaoh let our ancestors go from Egypt, they were forced to flee in great haste. They had not time to bake their bread; they could not wait for the yeast to rise. So the sun

beating down on the dough as they carried it along baked it into a flat, unleavened bread.''

The matzo was the "bread of affliction" which enabled the Chosen people to be delivered from slavery.

On this night the followers of Christ recall that before Jesus distributed the bread to all the disciples, he added the significant words that we hear in the Eucharistic celebration. Through this action all are able to become one in Christ, as Paul says:

"The fact that there is only one loaf means that, though there are many of us, we form a single body because we all share in this one loaf." (*I Corinthians* 10:17)

(The father now takes a matzo and breaks off a portion. He passes the matzo around and each eats a portion of it.)

Child:	Why did Jesus and his disciples drink wine at the Last Supper?
Leader:	The feast of the Passover begins and ends with the drinking of a cup of wine. It is both a blessing and a thanksgiving expressed in this benediction prayer:
Father:	Blessed are you, O Lord our God, King of the universe, creator of the fruit of the earth; you have given us this bread and wine to offer.

(All present take a sip of wine.)

Leader:	On this night the followers of Jesus read in the gospel according to *Luke:*
All:	"When the hour came he took his place at table, and the apostles with him. And he said to them, 'I have longed to eat this passover with you before I suffer; because, I tell you, I shall not eat it again until it is fulfilled in the kingdom of God.'

Then taking the cup, he gave thanks and said, 'Take this and share it among you, because from now on I tell you, I shall not drink wine until the kingdom of God comes.'

Then he took some bread, and when he had given thanks, broke it and gave it to them, saying, 'This is my body which will be given for you; do this as a memorial of me.'

He did the same with the cup after supper, and said, 'This cup is the new covenant in my blood which will be poured out for you.' " (*Luke* 22:15-20)

Leader:	For the Christian, then, this is the night of the new Passover. Let us recall with respect the feast of the Passover and its place in God's providence. Let us recall with gratitude how on this night Jesus introduced a new memorial for his followers. By this act and by his death and resurrection, he established a new sacrifice, a new deliverance.

V. THE CONCLUDING HALLEL (PSALM 118)

Leader:	We shall all join in reciting the concluding psalm of the *Hallel,* keeping in mind that Matthew tells us:

"After psalms had been sung, they left for the Garden of Olives." (*Matthew* 26:30)

PSALM 118
(Alternate verses between men and boys, and women and girls)

Alleluia!
Give thanks to Yahweh for Yahweh is good,
Yahweh's love is everlasting!
Let the House of Israel say it,
Yahweh's love is everlasting!

Let the House of Aaron say it,
Yahweh's love is everlasting!
Let those who fear Yahweh say it,
Yahweh's love is everlasting!

Hardpressed, I invoke Yahweh,
Yahweh heard me and came to my relief.
With Yahweh on my side, I fear nothing:
what can anyone do to me?

I would rather take refuge in Yahweh
than rely on people;
I would rather take refuge in Yahweh
than rely on princes.

I was pressed, pressed about to fall,
but Yahweh came to my help;
Yahweh is my strength and my song,
Yahweh has been my savior.

No, I shall not die, I shall live
to recite the deeds of Yahweh.
Though Yahweh has tried me often,
Yahweh has not abandoned me to death.

Open the gates of virtue to me,
I will come in and give thanks to Yahweh.
This is Yahweh's gateway
through which the virtuous may enter.

You are my God, I give you thanks,
I extol you, my God;
I give you thanks for having heard me,
you have been my savior.

All: Give thanks to Yahweh, for Yahweh is good,
Yahweh's love is everlasting!

Leader: We have heard God's Word; we have shared a Paschal meal of the Old Covenant and the New Covenant, and we share the great gift of Jesus to us: his body and blood in bread and wine, in each other. For where two or three are gathered in Jesus' name, he is also present. Now let us go in the peace and love of Jesus, who is the Christ.

All: Thanks Be To God!

VI. FINAL SONG

(All sing: melody: "When the Saints Go Marching In." Words are pronounced phonetically) (Loose translation: When peace will come, we can return to the Promised Land.)

VUKSHAY YAVO, YAVO SHALOM
VUKSHAY YAVO, YAVO SHALOM
AS BARAKIVET NEESA I'DEMESEK
VUKSHAY YAVO, YAVO SHALEM!

(Developed in collaboration with Dean Dolan and adapted in part from Arlene Hynes. The Passover Meal: A Ritual For Christian Homes. Paulist Press, 1972.)

Easter to Pentecost

Easter Symbols and Customs

Easter is the Church's greatest feast. The mystery we celebrate at this time is at the very heart of our faith: Jesus, after his death on the cross, has risen from the tomb and we will too because he did. Joy and victory are the key themes of the Easter Vigil and Easter Sunday liturgies. The only adequate expression for these days is the often repeated: ALLELUIA!

The Sunrise Service

The sun has a natural significance which connects it with the Resurrection theme. Early peoples attributed to the sun a great power because it dispelled darkness and brought the new day. This is also true of Christ, for he has dispelled the darkness of evil and sin to bring a new day of truth and life.

The Gospel writers narrate the Resurrection of Jesus as happening near dawn, linking the natural symbol with the central belief of Christianity.

Easter Lilies

The Easter lily is larger than the more generally known Madonna lily. It was introduced in Bermuda (from Japan) at the middle of the last century. In 1882 the florist W.K. Harris brought it to the United States and spread its use here. Since it flowers first around Easter time in this part of the world, it soon came to be called the Easter lily. The American public immediately accepted the implied suggestion and made it a symbolic feature of the Easter decoration on Easter day, and people adopted it as a favorite in their homes for the Easter solemnities.

Although the Easter lily did not directly originate from a religious symbolism, it has acquired that symbolism, and quite appropriately so. Its radiant whiteness, the delicate beauty of shape and its bugle form, make it an eloquent herald of the Easter celebration. Lilies have always been symbols of beauty, perfection and goodness, and so appear in the holy scriptures, both the Hebrew and the Christian Testaments, bearing this symbolism.

Jesus once showed his disciples some lilies and said, "Not even Solomon in all his glory was arrayed like one of these." (*Matthew* 6:28). Now, since Jesus himself stated that lilies are more glorious than the greatest earthly splendor, is it not fitting that we use these beautiful flowers to commemorate his glory on the day of his Resurrection?

Easter Eggs

In the ancient times eggs were a symbol of spring and fertility. An egg seems dead and yet contains new life; so does the earth at the end of winter. This is the reason why people in pre-Christian ages presented each other with eggs at the beginning of spring (which in those days also was the beginning of the new year).

In medieval times the eating of eggs was prohibited during Lent. So the faithful transferred the custom of giving eggs to Easter Sunday. Instead of representing fertility, the Easter egg now became a symbol of the rock tomb out of which our Lord gloriously emerged to the new life of his Resurrection. The Church even has a ritual blessing for eggs.

We decorate the eggs with many of the symbols described previously.

Blessing the Easter Eggs

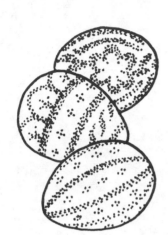

The whole household gathers to bless the eggs on Easter. All extend their hands over the eggs as one member of the household prays the blessing:

We praise you, O God, for these signs of life, our Easter eggs. We thank you for the bright, bursting forth of Christ our Lord. Amen. Alleluia!

In the same way, the household can bless the Easter pastries:

We praise you, O God, for sweetness and delight. We thank you for the journey of Lent. We rejoice in the resurrection of Christ and this Eastertime. Amen. Alleluia!

Easter Water

In the liturgy of Holy Saturday night, the presiding priest solemnly blesses the Easter water, which will be used during the service for baptisms. Families can take home a small container of this holy water to be used during the Easter season for family blessings on persons, house and rooms, Easter symbols such as eggs, pastry, baskets, meals. Each sprinkling signifies that all of our life is being baptized or being made holy by the presence of Christ to us.

During the year, parents can sign their children with a blessing using the holy water before tucking them into bed.

Family Paschal Candle

Burn a large white candle in your home at Eastertime, just as the Easter candle lights the sanctuary at church during Eastertime. Decorate it with the traditional symbols that are on the Paschal Candle, or any Christian or springtime symbols the family would like to have on their candle (nail polish or acrylic paints work best for this).

The Easter Candle is inscribed with an *alpha* (the beginning of the Greek alphabet) and an *omega* (the last letter, the end) with a cross in between. The four quarters of the cross are identified with the numerals of the current year.

Put your candle in a prominent place and you will have your very own Easter Candle to remind you that Christ is our light.

Blessing for the Candle: After the candle is decorated and put in place, the head of the household can pray a blessing on the candle while all family members extend their hands over the candle:

Loving God, we ask your blessing on this symbol of Christ our Light. May it be a constant reminder to all of us that we, too, are to bring the Light of Christ to others by our lives of justice and kindness. Amen.

In Greece it is a custom after the Easter Vigil to carry the "light" from the Easter Candle home to light the lamps in each home. All our light comes from the one light—Christ. Your family may wish to carry a light from the Easter Candle home to light your family Easter Candle for the first time. (A glass enclosed votive candle works well for this "transport.")

Easter Bunny

Hares and rabbits served our pre-Christian ancestors as symbols of fertility because they multiply so fast. They were kept in the homes and given as presents at the beginning of spring. From this ancient custom developed the story of the "Easter bunny" in Germany, in the fifteenth century. Little children believe that Easter eggs are produced and brought by the Easter bunny. This is one of the traditional fairy tales which delight the small children. It had no deep meaning, nor any religious background. In fact, the Easter bunny has never assumed religious symbolism like the Easter egg. Neither in liturgy nor in folklore do we find these animals connected with the spiritual significance of the Easter season, and there is no special blessing for rabbits or hares in the Roman Ritual.

Easter Lamb Cake

The Easter Lamb, representing Christ, with the flag of victory, is one of the most significant symbols of the festive season. It may be seen in pictures and images in the homes of most families in Catholic parts of Europe. The liturgical use of the Paschal Lamb as a symbol for the Risen Christ inspired the faithful of medieval times to eat lamb meat on Easter Sunday.

For further explanation of the tradition behind the symbol, refer to the earlier described Seder or Paschal meal.

Easter Pastry

In many countries of Europe people serve traditional breads and pastries at Easter like the Russian Easter bread *(Paska),* the German Easter loaves (Osterstollen), the Polish Easter cake *(Baba Wielanocna),* etc. Very often these breads and pastries, together with meat and eggs, are blessed by the priest on Holy Saturday. An Italian custom is to make a simple sweet bread dough shaped in the form of a chick, bunny, or doll. These breads are baked with a whole egg placed in the "tummy" of the form and frosted with egg yolk. The whole family is involved in the making of these Easter breads. They are brought to the Easter Vigil to be blessed and are given as gifts on Easter Sunday to young friends and relatives.

The Easter Food Basket

The blessing of the food, *Swiecone,* is a Polish custom performed on Holy Saturday. (All food which a Polish family eats on Easter Day is blessed by the priest.) This breakfast is called *Swiecone.* The egg, the symbol of life, is broken and shared with an exchange of good wishes. The Polish people have no special menu for Easter Day. There are no courses. Food aplenty is arranged upon sprigs of green leaves. Unlike Christmas, which is a day of family gathering, Easter in Poland is an occasion of traditional Polish hospitality when everybody is invited and welcomed. Perhaps this is the origin of our Easter Egg basket.

Easter Clothes

The tradition of wearing new dresses and apparel on Easter Sunday is practiced by many people in this country, even by those who otherwise pay little attention to the spiritual side of the feast. This custom goes back to the early centuries of Christianity.

The early Christians, most of whom were adults when they were baptized during the solemn Easter vigil on the night of Holy Saturday, used to wear white gowns throughout the whole Easter week as a symbol of their new life, pure and holy before God. The other Christians, who had already been baptized in previous years, did not wear white garments, but they dressed in new clothes at Easter to indicate that they, too, had risen to a new life in Christ, had put off the old way and put on Jesus' way. Thus the wearing of new things at Easter was an external profession and symbol of the Easter grace, of a spiritual resurrection to a better and holier life.

Emmaus Day: Monday After Easter

Luke's gospel (24:13-25) tells the story of the two disciples on their way from Jerusalem to Emmaus and how they meet a stranger. The stranger asks them why they are so sad, and they tell him about the execution of Jesus. So the three walk on together and the stranger explains to them about Jesus and why he had to die in order to rise. Finally, they dine together at Emmaus, and as they break bread the two disciples recognize that the stranger was Jesus: "It is the Lord!" In their sadness they had not been able to recognize him.

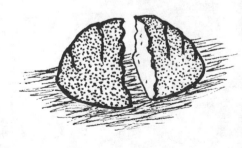

Celebrating Emmaus Day (Easter Monday) in your house might go like this: List four places that you've always said "Someday we must go there," but you have never gone, e.g., the zoo, the museum, a lake, a special restaurant, an old friend's or a distant relative's, a park.

Now make a family decision about your goal for this year's Emmaus Day outing. (If Easter Monday is not a good day, also decide on a date.) Talk about who will do what to be ready.

Before setting out, read together *Luke* 24:13-35. Then, with a little traveling music, set out. If possible, take a kind of transportation that will be special: walking, bicycling, taking the bus. Make the trip something of a storytelling time, warning everyone ahead of time to have a story to share. (Adapted from *Major Feasts and Seasons* Vol. 2, No. 2)

Daily Prayer

The arrival of Easter is not the time to discontinue the good beginnings experienced during Lent, particularly the time set aside for prayer. Eastertime has its own way of praying together. Following are some suggestions:

Morning Prayer: Face east toward the rising sun. Raise arms to shoulder level, palms up. Then, with head up, raise arms slowly above head saying: Glory to the Father

Glory to Jesus

Glory to the Spirit.

Slowly lower your arms and conclude with: "May God watch over us and bless us today."

Evening Prayer: Mom or Dad could begin by thanking God for the blessings of the day. Children will soon add to the prayer of thanks. Another night it might be a prayer for others, a prayer of forgiveness, a prayer of praise, etc. If this is done consistently, in time all of those prayer forms will become part of the family night prayer. This is also a good time to begin teaching the little ones some of our traditional memorized prayers.

Sit quietly for awhile and watch the setting sun. If you have a copy of the record, play the sunset theme from Ferde Grofe's *Grand Canyon Suite.*

Mealtime Prayer: Mealtime is a good time to begin spontaneous prayer in your home. But spontaneous prayer can become as repetitious as memorized prayer with children. If this is the case, try making and using a family prayer wheel.

Cut a round circle out of heavy cardboard. Draw pie-shaped wedges on it. On each of these sections, print the family's suggestions for prayer. With a brad, attach an arrow in the center of the circle so that the arrow spins freely. Each day before the family meal, someone spins the arrow to select the prayer suggestion for that day. Anyone may add to the prayer in keeping with the chosen suggestion.

A Springtime Nature Walk

A springtime nature walk is a good family activity that will provide an opportunity for the family to witness the renewal of life on the natural level. Plan your nature walk for a mild day, allow plenty of time, and if possible, go to a nearby park or wooded area to which you can return later to observe additional seasonal changes.

Look for violets, ferns and grasses sprouting from between dead leaves; note tree branches about to bloom; look and listen for toads, birds, and insects. Sniff!

Bring a box or bag so you can take home some small signs of new life. You can display these later as a table centerpiece or help the children make a simple dish garden or terrarium with mosses, grasses and blossoming branches.

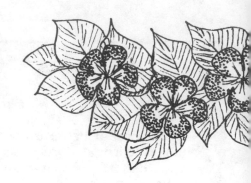

The Fortieth Day   Ascension Day

Read the first chapter of *Acts*. Spend some time looking at the clouds (sprawl on the ground for this). Clouds in our scriptures and in the religion of many other peoples have a closeness to God because they are so like spirits. They are felt to be a hovering presence of the Lord.

The Fiftieth Day   Pentecost

Read the second chapter of *Acts*. On Pentecost, those folks heard a wind, they breathed deeply, they felt the presence of God swirling about them and filling their very selves. They knew the Spirit when it happened to them!

So today we celebrate this wonderful way to know the closeness of God: the God manifest in the breezes and the wind storms of the earth, the God manifest in our own breathing. Celebrate! Blow, breathe, inhale, exhale, hold your breath, run out of breath, chase the wind, blow hard, inspire, expire, puff, gasp, wheeze, whistle, fly kites, blow soap bubbles, play wind instruments, make pin wheels, receive the Holy Spirit!

(Adapted from *Major Feasts and Seasons.* Vol. 2, No. 2)

Apples

For a family harvest festival, take one whole day and go to an apple orchard where you can pick your own. Learn to tell one kind of apple from another (a Delicious from a Winesap or a Jonathon from a McIntosh). Discover your favorites for eating. Bring back many kinds and have an all-apple meal: cider, dumplings for the main course, pie for dessert.

Before your apple meal, or just after you've picked a beautiful bushel, gather in a circle and all extend hands over the apples to bless them. "Blessed are you, O Lord our God, ruler of the universe, for giving us the fruit of the apple tree."

Then each person picks an apple, all together say the alphabet as each turns the stem. When a stem breaks, the alphabet is interrupted for a moment and that person praises God for something beginning with the letter the stem broke on. Continue reciting the alphabet until another

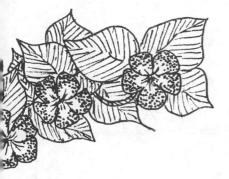

person's apple stem breaks off, and a prayer of praise is offered.

Save your appleseeds! Later that night, spread them out on the table and tell the story of John Chapman who got to be known as Johnny Appleseed—a real hero of the American frontier who had friends of all colors and carried only the bible and his appleseeds.

At bedtime say this prayer: "Keep us, O Lord, as the apple of your eye!"

Leaves

On the day you rake your yard, make the biggest pile of leaves you've ever seen. High! Wide! Deep! Get as many people as possible to jump into the leaf pile. Take a few favorite leaves to the family dinner table, arrange them in the center and listen to a recording of "Autumn Leaves." Share hot cocoa and toasted marshmallows, if leaf burning is permitted where you live. Then each person hold up a leaf and pray a prayer of praise and thanks for autumn's beauty, and the day's fun.

All Saints—November 1

This is *our* day, the day when we celebrate the household called Church. How about a neighborhood or block progressive dinner—Salad at one home, main course at another, dessert at another and so on? As you progress from house to house, the whole group could sing: "When the Saints Go Marching In."

(Adapted from the Liturgical Conference)

All Souls—November 2

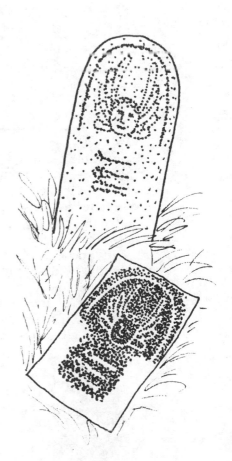

Early in November we have a day for remembering all the dead. One way to do this would be to visit a cemetery. Take along some large pieces of paper and some crayons. Make rubbings on the grave stones, especially the very old ones. (Rubbings are made by placing a piece of paper on the stone, holding it still while rubbing all over it with the crayon. The paper then shows the words and designs of the stone). Notice the poems on some of the stones, the loving words on others, the dates that show the age of the person.

Cemeteries are often beautiful places for a picnic. In some countries, people bring the favorite foods of a friend or relative who has died and have the picnic near the grave. It is a way of remembering how special each person was. At home the rubbings can decorate the wall during November.

(Adapted from Liturgical Conference)

A Victory Book

Make a beautifully decorated list of those who have died whom you want to remember in prayer throughout the month—relatives, neighbors, friends, people who were famous, people whom no one else remembers. This, too, can be made large enough to become a wall decoration that will act as a reminder for the family.

(Adapted from Liturgical Conference)

November Menu Special

Doughnuts are a special November food—the circle reminds us of the circle of life and death: the seed springs to life, grows, matures, produces its fruit with new seeds, dies. But now there is a new seed. The circle has no end. Make doughnuts as a family and enjoy eating them together.

Christ, the King

This feast, which follows the Sundays of Pentecost deserves a special dessert: a bundt cake decorated like a crown in honor of Christ the King. (The cake can be decorated with colored gumdrops for jewels in the crown, the cake itself is crown-shaped.) Let the children help with the decoration of the cake.

Before eating the cake, pray Psalm 97 together: "The Lord is King! Let the earth rejoice and everyone be glad!"

Campaign for Human Development Dinner

The week of the Campaign for Human Development can become more personal for your family. Choose one day during the week when you have a meal comparable to the meals usually eaten by nearly two-thirds of the world's people. Have your family share a meal which costs no more than two dollars for the whole family, or share a meal of rice and bread. Then give the money saved on food that day to the Campaign for Human Development.

A Family Ritual for Thanksgiving

Some time between now and Thanksgiving have the family gather together to decorate a small box with an autumn or Thanksgiving motif. Make a slot in the cover of the box and decorate it in such a way so that it is free to be opened easily.

After the box is decorated, give each person in the family as many small pieces of paper as there are family members. Have each person write the special gift that each family member contributes to the rest of the family. Fold the paper and write the name of that person on the outside of the folded paper (e.g., Mom—bakes great pies, Oscar—the peacemaker of the family). Teens and parents can help preschoolers write theirs. If others are sharing Thanksgiving with you, include their names and gifts as well.

Use the box as the focal point of your Thanksgiving centerpiece. Then, just before the food is served (while it is all keeping warm in the oven), gather the family around the already set table, open the box and allow time for each person to read the papers with his/her name on them. Have someone in the family lead a prayer of thanks for the family, for the gifts present in the family, and then invite others to add whatever else for which they are thankful.

When the prayer is over, go to the kitchen as a family, where each person is given something to carry to the table for dinner.

Bibliography of Resources

(Addresses of publishers follow in last section of bibliography)

I Program Resources

Coleman, Bill and Patty. TOTAL PARISH FAMILY PROGRAM. Twenty-Third Publications, 1979. This program is comprised of two units. Unit I—*Together in Prayer.* Unit 2—*Together with Jesus.* Each unit contains teacher booklets and duplicator master activity sheets covering preschool through adult levels plus a family take-home book. TPFP is designed to involve all members of the family at their own learning levels. Step-by-step directions make this program clear and easy to follow.

Curran, Dolores. TALKS WITH PARENTS. James Alt, Publisher, Green Bay, WI. A weekly column for parents. Parishes ordering for 12 months or more: $4.00 per month. Less than one year: $5.00 per month. Cost entitles purchaser to reproduce copy. Can be used in the parish bulletin, for sacramental preparation, adult education classes. Articles sent on ready-to-reproduce 5 ½ x 8 ½ cards.

FAMILY CLUSTERING, INC. Resources, consultation and training for all interested in developing Family Cluster model. Write for further information.

FAMILY LEARNING TEAMS, INC. Resources, consultation and training available. The training offers curriculum materials, floating introductory workshops and consultation for the implementation and sustenance of family learning teams in parishes.

FAMILY MINISTRY: RESOURCES FOR DIOCESAN IMPLEMENTATION. United States Catholic Conference, 1978. Includes the Bishop's Pastoral on the Family, *Sounds of the Family* (a pastoral listening and planning workbook) and resources for organization, ministry and leadership development at the diocesan and parish level.

FAMILY: PARISH RELIGIOUS EDUCATION PROGRAM. Paulist Press. A total package for instruction, experience, and celebration. Each kit contains slides, filmstrips, transparencies, cassettes, and printed material for intergenerational sessions on eight themes. Cycles A, B, C, D, E available. Reduced cost when buying three or more.

FATE II. The Liturgical Conference, 1980. A Lenten/Eastertime packet for involving the total parish, including ideas for families, in an experience of the season and in parish renewal based on the model of the Revised Rite of Christian Initiation. (Initially published in 1974 under the title FROM ASHES TO EASTER.)

Heisberger, Jean Marie (ed.). CHANGE MY HEART: FAMILY LENTEN HANDBOOK. Paulist Press, 1977. Different approaches for family prayer during Lent. Home customs, Way of the Cross, evening prayer, Seder Meal, and home liturgy. The last section, *Life in Life,* is an adult discussion series for Lent to be used as a component of CHANGE MY HEART.

Hilliard, Dick. THE LORD BLESSES ME. Resource Publications, 1978. Celebrations of God's Word for children and families. Patterned after the "Learning Center" concept, the celebrations in this book were developed in response to the need for para-sacramental services for children and young families. Each celebration suggests many activities which introduce people to the celebrational aspects of Christian Liturgy. More than forty celebrations based on the Sunday readings for Advent, Christmas, Lent and Holy Week.

MAJOR FEASTS AND SEASONS. The Liturgical Conference, 1975-77. Eight seasonal packets designed to help parish teams plan for major liturgical seasons. Each packet contains a section for home celebrations.

Nutt, Grady. FAMILY TIME: A REVOLUTIONARY OLD IDEA, Family Communication Committee of the Million Dollar Round Table, 1976. Suggestions for spending quality time as a family. Suggestions include Sharetime, Activitytime, and Outingtime.

Otto, Herbert A. THE FAMILY CLUSTER: A MULTI-BASE ALTERNATIVE. Holistic Press, 1975. A manual for use by families who wish to develop their own cluster.

PARISH FAMILY MINISTRY RESOURCES. United States Catholic Conference, 1979. Includes *Models of Ministry,* describing ways 30 parishes minister to families and make a difference.

In addition to the individual works listed above, several publishers offer Family catechetical programs and/or program resources. Write the following for their catalogue of family resources—Alternatives; Augsburg Publishing House; Christian Family Movement; Church of the Latter Day Saints (Mormons); Claretian Publications; Concordia Publishing House; Discipleship Resources; Families For Prayer; Gospel Light Publications; Griggs Educational Service; National Marriage Encounter; Paulist Press; Pennant Educational Materials ("Valuing in the Family"); Sadlier; Seabury Press; St. Mary's College Press; Twenty-Third Publications; Winston Press.

II Books

Barbeau, Clayton (ed.) FUTURE OF THE FAMILY. Glencoe Publishing Co. Inc., 1971. Series of articles on the family "in transition." Authors include Joseph and Lois Bird, Sidney Callahan, Rosemary Haughton, Paul Marx, etc.

Bosco, Antoinette. SUCCESSFUL SINGLE PARENTING. Twenty-Third Publications, 1978. The author has been the sole parent of six children for the past 12 years. She discusses coping with the transition trauma, experiencing powerlessness, problems of authority, sex, and going beyond survival. Good for those who want to support the single parent.

Bushnell, Horace. VIEWS OF CHRISTIAN NURTURE AND SUBJECTS RELATED THERETO. Scholars, Facsimiles, and Reprints, 1975. (Originally published in 1847 under the title *Christian Nurture*). A catechetical classic worth reading for its contemporary views of the role of the family in Christian nurture.

Curran, Dolores. IN THE BEGINNING THERE WERE THE PARENTS. Winston Press, 1978. Although this is a book written to parents, its style is also challenging to the DRE in terms of the parents' role in catechesis.

Dixon, Dorothy. THE FORMATIVE YEARS. Twenty-Third Publications, 1978. Highlights intellectual, emotional, spiritual and physical stages of development in early years. Excellent background for teachers and parents.

Girzaitis, Loretta. THE CHURCH AS RE-FLECTING COMMUNITY: MODELS OF ADULT RELIGIOUS LEARNING. Twenty-Third Publications, 1977. An information-packed volume for the adult and family catechist, this book contains a chapter on the family. Three commentary articles on the family and family ministry are contained in a chapter supplement. Also many resource suggestions.

Harris, Maria (ed.). PARISH RELIGIOUS EDUCATION. Paulist Press, 1978. A collection of articles that focus on the practical and theoretical aspects of parish religious education, including family religious education.

Hovda, Robert. DRY BONES. The Liturgical Conference, 1973. A collection of essays providing background for the planning and celebrating of rituals.

Howard, Jane. FAMILIES. Simon and Schuster, 1978. A collection of stories based on personal interviews about a variety of family types and styles which helps break through the myth of the nuclear family.

Huck, Gabe and Virginia Sloyan (ed.) PARISHES AND FAMILIES. The Liturgical Conference, 1973. Theoretical and practical ideas to aid Christian formation of families through ritual.

Huck, Gabe and Elizabeth Jeep. CELEBRATE SUMMER: A GUIDEBOOK FOR CONGREGATIONS. Paulist Press, 1973. Planners for activities and prayer services will find this helpful for family-oriented celebrations and liturgies during the summer months.

Illich, Ivan. DESCHOOLING SOCIETY. Harper & Row, 1972. AFTER DE-SCHOOLING WHAT? Harper & Row, 1973. A radical proposal for changing our institutional structures.

Jones, Paul D. REDISCOVERING RITUAL. Paulist Press, 1973. The theory of ritual and six ritual events for individuals and groups.

Keniston, Kenneth and the Carnegie Council on Children. ALL OUR CHILDREN: THE AMERICAN FAMILY UNDER PRESSURE. Harcourt, Brace, 1978. The authors propose a program of social reform that can counteract the social and economic pressures faced by the American family today, which when reformed, the authors feel, the family can survive more healthily.

Koehler, George E. LEARNING TOGETHER: A GUIDE FOR INTERGENERATIONAL EDUCATION IN THE CHURCH. Discipleship Resources, 1977. A guide for intergenerational learning. Includes chapters explaining the IG approach and ways to get started; special problem areas, planning, units that have been used by groups, and resources. A product of the United Methodist Church.

McBride, Angela Barron. CONTRADICTIONS OF A MARRIED FEMINIST. Harper & Row, 1977. How does one care about traditional values and still own a feminist ideology? This is a penetrating study of that kind of conflict. Personal, yet well documented.

Mitchell, Leonel L. THE MEANING OF RITUAL. Paulist Press, 1977. A basic introduction to the meaning and history of ritual in Western Christianity, and an examination of its place in human life.

Moran, Gabriel. DESIGN FOR RELIGION. Seabury Press, 1971. Suggests a new framework for the Church's approach to religious education. Emphasizes the adult as primary subject of religious education.

_____. VISION AND TACTICS: TOWARD AN ADULT CHURCH. Seabury Press, 1968. Discusses the vision that contemporary theology can provide for religious education and describes some concrete steps in that process.

Nelson, C. Ellis. WHERE FAITH BEGINS. John Knox Press, 1976. Main contention is that religion at its deepest levels is located within a person's sentiments and is a result of the way a person has been socialized by the adults who cared for him/her as a child.

Nouwen, Henri. CREATIVE MINISTRY. Doubleday, 1971. Ministry in the Church is seen as pastoral activities to be integrated. The chapter on education is particularly apropos.

O'Neil, Robert and Michael Donovan. CHILDREN, CHURCH AND GOD. Corpus Publications, 1970. The authors present their case against formal religious education. Out of print but worth finding a copy.

Otto, Herbert A. MARRIAGE AND FAMILY ENRICHMENT: NEW PERSPECTIVES AND PROGRAMS. Abingdon Press, 1976. A survey and sampling of 19 representative programs. Includes procedures, philosophy, and extensive resources. A handbook that gives an overview of the whole movement.

PACE. Volumes 1 ff. St. Mary's College Press. Articles on various aspects of family catechesis as well as other aspects of parish ministry.

Pottebaum, Gerard. THE RITES OF PEOPLE. The Liturgical Conference, 1975. The theory of ritual and the sacredness of the rituals people share naturally.

RITUALS FOR A NEW DAY. Parthenon Press, 1976. A creation of the Alternate Rituals Projects of the Section on Worship of the Board of Discipleship of the United Methodist Church. A collection of rituals of passage.

Reardon, Mary and Sr. Suzanne LaChapelle, RSM. FAMILY RETREAT PROGRAM. Twenty-Third Publications, 1979. A step-by-step guide for an overnight (or two afternoons) retreat. Includes details for meals and activities for each age group.

Satir, Virginia. PEOPLEMAKING. Science and Behavior Books, 1972. A useful, clear book for families who want to improve their relationships, their self-image and communication skills.

Thompson, Fred. CELEBRATIONS FOR CHILDREN. Twenty-Third Publications, 1979. A step-by-step guide and practical aid to introduce children to good liturgy.

Westerhoff, John H. A COLLOQUY ON CHRISTIAN EDUCATION. Pilgrim Press, 1972.
_____. GENERATION TO GENERATION: CONVERSATIONS ON RELIGIOUS EDUCATION AND CULTURE (with Gwen Kennedy Neville). Pilgrim Press, 1974.
_____. LEARNING THROUGH LITURGY (with Gwen Kennedy Neville). Seabury Press, 1978.
_____. VALUES FOR TOMORROW'S CHILDREN. Pilgrim Press, 1970.
_____. WILL OUR CHILDREN HAVE FAITH? Seabury Press, 1976. Westerhoff contends that we need to make systematic efforts toward using socialization as the context for religious growth and learning, that there should be an end to the schooling-instruction method of religious education, and that the interplay between the liturgical process and the processes of education, coupled with the insights of anthropology and folk rituals have a large part to play in the religious growth of people and families. Best read in order of publication.

III Audio-Cassettes and Audio-Visuals

A number of audio-cassette tapes and audio-visual programs are available to the catechist on the subject of family catechesis and family ministry. Write the following publishers for information: National Catholic Reporter Cassettes; New Life Films; St. Anthony Messenger Tapes; St. Thomas More Cassettes; Twenty-Third Publications.

IV Periodicals

ALTERNATIVE: AN ALTERNATIVE LIFESTYLE NEWSLETTER, Alternative, (quarterly). Explores simpler ways to live through alternatives celebrations. Concerned with education, health, food, housing, economics, new visions of family life.

BRINGING RELIGION HOME, Claretian Publications (monthly). A newsletter for busy parents with helps for creating a religious atmosphere in the home—family prayer, home religious practice, idea exchange, and resource listings.

THE CATECHIST, Peter Li, Inc. (monthly during school year). Articles and features address catechetical concerns.

FAMILY LIFE TODAY, Gospel Light Publications (monthly). Articles on marriage, communication, teenagers as well as a "family time" feature.

LIVING LIGHT, William H. Sadlier, Inc. Theoretical articles and working papers on catechesis.

MARRIAGE AND FAMILY LIVING, Abbey Press (monthly). Popular style and format addressing a variety of issues dealing with all aspects of family life. Includes the monthly feature "Family Night."

MARRIAGE ENCOUNTER, National Marriage Encounter (monthly). Contains articles on couple and family growth. Material and questions for dialogue and enrichment. National Marriage Encounter news and focus.

MODERN LITURGY, Resource Publications (monthly). Articles and practical suggestions on liturgy and ritualizing in the parish. Vol. 5, No. 4 is totally on family liturgy.

MUSHROOM FAMILY, Pittsburgh, PA. (quarterly). Useful and creative ideas for improving the family environment. Thoughtful and good resource.

NATIONAL BULLETIN ON LITURGY, Publications Service (5 times a year). A pastoral liturgy bulletin. Each issue features a particular aspect of liturgy. Vol. 12, No. 68, March-April, 1979 is entirely on Family Prayer.

RELIGIOUS EDUCATION, The Religious Education Association of U.S. and Canada (bi-monthly). Research papers and articles in catechetical ministry.

RELIGION TEACHER'S JOURNAL, Twenty-Third Publications (monthly during school year). Articles and features on classroom catechesis as well as family catechesis. Practical ideas that can be modified for family programs.

TODAY'S PARISH, Twenty-Third Publications (monthly during school year). Articles and features address total parish life and ministries.

A family program can provide one of the best means of integrating the parish ministries of community building, prayer and worship, social action, pastoral care, and education.

————————V Resources For Parents————————

Berends, Polly Berrien. WHOLE PARENT/ WHOLE CHILD. Harper & Row, 1975. Subtitled *A Spiritual and Practical Guide to the First Four Years of Parenthood.* A spiritual basis for love and authority in the parental years. Offers practical guidelines for toys, books, scripture, sacramental preparation and sex education.

Bird, Joseph and Lois. POWER TO THE PARENTS. Doubleday, 1974. A common sense approach to parenting that challenges parents to be the thoughtful, caring leaders that their children need.

Briggs, Dorothy C. YOUR CHILD'S SELF- ESTEEM. Doubleday, 1975. Children's perception of themselves is the basis for good mental health. How the parent can help create feelings of self-worth is the central challenge of parenthood.

Brusselmans, Christiane. A PARENT'S GUIDE: RELIGION FOR LITTLE CHIL- DREN. Our Sunday Visitor, Inc., 1977. (Revised and expanded edition) This popular volume talks about religious formation from baptism through the early years. A practical, clear approach that includes the "77 questions" children ask most.

Carson, Rachel. A SENSE OF WONDER, Harper & Row, 1965. A classic "must" for parents and children. What it means to have a sense of mystery and awe of God's creation. How we share that gift.

Curran, Dolores. AND THEN GOD MADE FAMILIES. Alt-Curran Associates, 1977.
————. FAMILY PRAYER. Twenty-Third Publications, 1979.
————. IN THE BEGINNING THERE WERE THE PARENTS. Winston Press, 1978.
————. WHO, ME TEACH MY CHILD RELIGION? Winston Press, 1974. All of Ms. Curran's books come out of her own experience as a mother and religious educator. In her readable style, she gives strong

parental affirmation, down-to-earth advice, and resources for parents.

Coleman, Bill and Patty. TOGETHER IN PRAYER and TOGETHER WITH JESUS, Twenty-Third Publications, 1979. These books include prayers, scripture reflections, family activities.

Farrell, Melvin L. THEOLOGY FOR PAR- ENTS AND TEACHERS. Hi-Time Publications, 1972. Deals with the questions most frequently asked since Vatican II. Gives adult input on theological issues and offers understandable base for response.

Gordon, Dr. Thomas. P.E.T.: PARENT EF- FECTIVENESS TRAINING. Plume Books, 1975. Skills for better parenting. Emphasis on listening, issues of conflict and feelings.

Hover, Margot. A HAPPIER FAMILY, Vol. 1. Twenty-Third Publications, 1978. A book of practical suggestions to help families resolve difficulties and live together in harmony.
————. A HAPPIER FAMILY, Vol. 2. Twenty-Third Publications, 1979. More themes and aids for harmony in family living.
Larson, Earnest and Patricia Galvin. LITUR- GY BEGINS AT HOME. Liguori Publications, 1974. Shows how the foundations of good celebration are laid in religious formation in the home. Out of print, but worth finding a copy.

Working, Miji & Lois Bock. HAPPINESS IS A FAMILY TIME TOGETHER. Fleming H. Revell Co., 1975.
————. HAPPINESS IS A FAMILY WALK WITH GOD. Fleming H. Revell Co., 1977. Exercises for families to encourage sharing and self-disclosure. Themes include self-worth, God's love, growth, family background, future plans, knowing God, etc. Each sharing time also includes a "fun" activity and suggestions for informal prayer.

_____*VI Publishers and Addresses*_____

Abbey Press, St. Meinrad, IN 47577

Abingdon Press, 201-8th Ave. S., Nashville, TN 37202

Arena Lettres, 432 Park Ave. So., New York, NY 10016

Alternatives, 1924 E. 3rd St., Bloomington, IN 47401

Augsburg Publishing House, 426 S. 5th St., Minneapolis, MN 55415

Ave Maria Press, Notre Dame, IN 46556

Christian Family Movement, National Office, P.O. Box 792, Whiting, IN 46394

Church of the Latter Day Saints (Mormons) (Contact your local chapter)

Claretian Publications, 221 W. Madison St., Chicago, IL 60606

Concordia Publishing House, 3558 S. Jefferson Ave. St. Louis, MO 63118

Discipleship Resources, P.O. Box 840, Nashville, TN 37202

Family Clustering Inc., P.O. Box 18074, Twelve Corners Branch, Rochester, NY 14618

Family Enrichment Bureau, 1615 Ludington St., Escanaba, MI 49829

Families For Prayer, 773 Madison Ave., Albany, NY 12208

Family Learning Teams, Inc. National Training Center, P.O. Box 42, Mount Vernon, VA 22121

Fleming H. Revell Co., 184 Central Ave., Old Tappan, NJ 07675

Fides/Claretian, P.O. Box F., Notre Dame, IN 46556

Franciscan Communications Center, 1229 S. Santee Ave., Los Angeles, CA 90015

Glencoe Publishing C. Inc., 17337 Ventura Blvd., Encino, CA 91316

Gospel Light Publications, P.O. Box 1591, Glendale, CA 91204

Griggs Educational Service, 1731 Barcelona St., Livermore, CA 94550

Harcourt, Brace, Jovanovich, Inc., 757-3rd Ave., New York, NY 10017

Harper & Row Publishing C., 102-53rd St., New York, NY 10022

Hi-Time Publishers, Inc., Box 7337, Milwaukee, WI 53213

Holistic Press, Olympic Blvd., Beverly Hills, CA 90211

James Alt, Publisher, 300 Dauphin St., Green Bay, WI 54301

Liguori Publications, 1 Liguori Dr., Liguori, MO 63057

John Knox Press, 341 Ponce de Leon Ave. N.E., Rm 416, Atlanta, GA 30308

Liturgical Conference, 810 Rhode Island Ave. N.E., Washington, DC 20018

Living Light, 11 Park Place, New York, NY 10017

Mushroom Family, Box 12572, Pittsburgh, PA 15241

National Catholic Reporter Cassettes, Box 281, Kansas City, MO 64141

National Marriage Encounter, 955 Lake Dr., St. Paul, MN 55120

New Life Films, Inc., P.O. Box 2008, Kansas City, KA 66110

Our Sunday Visitor, Inc., 200 Noll Plaza, Huntington, IN 46750

Parthenon Books, 9808 Amanita Dr., Tujunga, CA 91042

Paulist Press, 545 Island Road, Ramsey, NJ 07446

Peter Li, Inc., 2451 E. River Rd., Dayton, OH 45439

Family programs are almost always community developers, and the people in the program who have experienced a community spirit on a smaller scale naturally help spread and develop that spirit in the larger community.

Pilgrim Press, 39 University Place, Princeton, NJ 08540

Religious Education, The Religious Education Association of U.S. and Canada, 409 Prospect St., New Haven, CT 06510

Resource Publications, P.O. Box 444, Saratoga, CA 95070

Sadlier, 11 Park Place, New York, NY 10007

Scholars, Facsimiles and Reprints, P.O. Box 344, Delmar, NY 12054

Science & Behavior Books Inc., P.O. Box 11457, Palo Alto, CA 94306

Seabury Press, 815 2nd. Ave., New York, NY 10017

Simon and Schuster, 1230 Ave. of the Americas, New York, NY 10020

St. Anthony Messenger Press, 1615 Republic St., Cincinnati, OH 45210

St. Mary's College Press, Winona, MN 44987

Thomas More Association, 180 N. Wabash Ave., Chicago, IL 60601

Twenty-Third Publications, P.O. Box 180, West Mystic, CT 06388

United States Catholic Conference, Department of Education, 1312 Massachusetts Ave. N.W., Washington, DC 20005

Winston Press, 430 Oak Grove, Suite 203, Minneapolis, MN 55403

The parish's greatest contribution to families is through its work with parents.
